GO FOR BEGINNERS

by
Iwamoto Kaoru, 9-dan

THE ISHI PRESS, INC.

Berkeley   Tokyo

Published by The Ishi Press, Inc.

CPO Box 2126, Tokyo, Japan
ISBN 0–87040–166–1

This and any other Ishi Press publication may be ordered from:

THE ISHI PRESS, INC., CPO Box 2126, Tokyo, Japan

First Printing July 1972
Second Printing May 1973
Printed in Japan
by
Sokosha Printing Co, Ltd.

TABLE OF CONTENTS

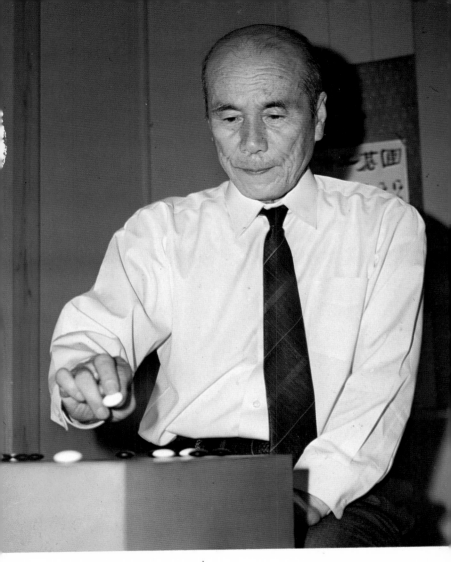

The author plays a stone.

A game of go in progress.

PREFACE

This is a book on the game of go for complete beginners. It is divided into two parts. The first part contains an introduction, a brief example game and a clear, leisurely explanation of the rules. The second part deals with the simplest techniques of good play which all players need to know. Many easy and some more difficult problems, which I hope the reader will try to work out for himself, are included as illustrations. A concise list of the rules can be found in the appendix, and a glossary gives the meaning and pronunciation of the more common technical go terms.

Go is a wonderful game, and I have devoted a lifetime to playing it and teaching it. I am happy to see it becoming popular in the western world, where I hope it will flourish as it has in Japan, Korea, and China.

I wish to express my thanks for the considerable help furnished by the staff of Ishi Press in the preparation of this manuscript.

Tokyo, March 5, 1972   Iwamoto Kaoru

PART
I

The Rules of Go

CHAPTER I: INTRODUCTION

Go is one of the most ancient, interesting, and rewarding of all board games. Originating in China, probably between four and five thousand years ago, it reached Japan during the seventh century A.D., where it has achieved its highest development. It was brought to Europe about one hundred years ago, and is now becoming popular there and in America.

As you can see from the photographs on the preceding color pages, go uses the simplest of elements—wood and stone, line and circle, black and white. It is played on a wooden board marked with nineteen vertical and nineteen horizontal lines. The pieces used are disks of black slate and white shell slightly more than two centimeters in diameter. These, even when made of plastic or glass, as in mass-produced sets, are called stones. They are played on the intersections formed by the lines on the board, not within the squares. The board is empty at the beginning of the game, and the two players take turns placing stones on it one at a time, one player playing black the other playing white. Once played, a stone remains in its place, not moving about from point to point.

Go is a territorial game. Each player tries to surround vacant areas on the board, which then become his territory. A player can also capture opposing stones by occupying all the points adjacent to them, but capturing stones is not the main purpose. The game is over when neither player can make any more territory or take any more prisoners, the winner being the one with the most territory.

The go board is not exactly square, but measures 41½ by 44½ centimeters, being placed with the narrow ends facing the two players so that the stones overlap slightly in the horizontal direction. This avoids the monotony of perfect squares, and the players often add to the effect by placing their stones somewhat off center. A stone, held between the index and middle fingers, is placed on the board decisively making a clear and solid click; the thicker the board and the heavier the stones, the more pleasing the sound.

Although the stones themselves do not move during the game there is always a feeling of powerful movement over the board; of advance and retreat, of growth and withering, of stability and change. In the shifting combat, a group of stones strong at one moment may be in desperate trouble a few moves later, or a stone which seemed thoroughly dead may suddenly spring to life with devastating effect. This is what makes go so subtle and fascinating, and why its players show it such devotion. A story goes that when the philosopher Hsuan-tzu lay on his deathbed he remarked to the people standing around him that if heaven should see fit to grant him another one hundred years of life, he would spend fifty of them playing go. To a really dedicated player this statement betrays a certain lack of enthusiasm for the game, but Hsuan-tzu was probably speaking to non-players and did not want them to think he had completely flipped out.

CHAPTER 2: DEMONSTRATION GAME

There is no better way to learn how go is played than to go through a short demonstration. For the sake of brevity, the game in this chapter takes place on a 9×9 board instead of the usual 19×19, but the rules of go are the same no matter what the size of the board. You can play through this game on a 9×9 go board, which can be made by masking off part of an ordinary board, or you can follow it by just looking at the diagrams. Since the stones do not move about, go diagrams are easy to read. In **Dia. 1**, ❶ is the first stone played, ② the second, and so on.

Besides getting a general idea of the game in this chapter, you will learn exactly what territory is, how it is formed, and how it is counted. You will also see how stones are captured, but we will be going into that matter in more detail in chapter 3.

Dia. 1   As always in go, Black plays first. You are free to put your stones wherever you like, but notice that the players here do not play right on the edges of the board, and will not start to do so until rather late in the game. This is a good policy.

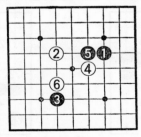

Dia. 1

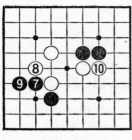

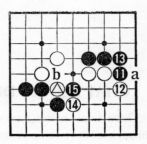

Dia. 2   Dia. 3

Dia. 2   With 7 and 9 Black begins to stake out some territory in the lower left corner.

Dia. 3   The area in the upper right corner starts to fall into Black's hands, too. It is bounded above and to the right by the edges of the board, and is walled off below by a solid row of black stones. It is still open to the left, and there is a small gap at the point marked 'a', but Black will deal with these matters in due time.

When Black plays 15 we are presented with an example of threatened capture, or **atari**. White △ has become surrounded on three sides by black stones, and if Black is permitted to play on the fourth side at 'b', White △ will be removed from the board.

Dia. 4   White saves his threatened stone by playing 16. Black 17 is another atari, this time against △, and White 18 is

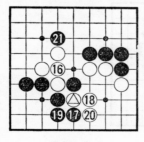

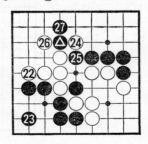

Dia. 4   Dia. 5

another saving move. The end of this diagram sees Black in control of the lower left corner, White in control of the lower right, and Black ambitiously stepping out to 21 on the upper side.

Dia. 5 White 22 threatens Black's whole structure in the lower left, although this is something which is not obvious except to an experienced player, and Black has to strengthen his position with 23. Now White counterattacks with 24 and 26, and the next diagram will witness the capture of Black ⬤ and 27.

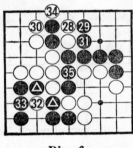

Dia. 6

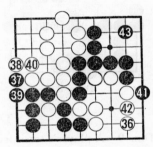

Dia. 7

Dia. 6 White captures the two black stones by playing 28, 30 and 34, removing them from the board and putting them in the upturned lid of his bowl when he plays 34. The two points where they rested have now become White's territory, along with a good many more in the upper left corner, while Black has walled off the upper right corner. White 32, which was played just to test Black's defenses, is in atari, being surrounded on three sides by Black 33, ⬤, and ⬤, and cannot hope for salvation. Black next plays 35, cutting off the white stones in the lower right corner and making them vulnerable.

Dia. 7 White defends his position with 36, and now both players begin to complete the walls around their territories by playing at the edges.

Dia. 8 At the end of this diagram all the boundaries are completed. Both players recognize that there is nothing more they can do to enlarge their own territories or to reduce their opponents', so the game is over. Let's count and see who has won.

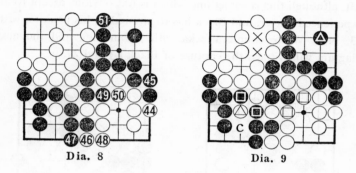

Dia. 8   Dia. 9

COUNTING

Dia. 9 A player's territory consists of the vacant points he has surrounded. In the upper right corner Black has surrounded nine points—see if you agree. The point ⚫ does not count, even though it is in the middle of Black's territory, because it is occupied by a black stone.

In the lower right corner White has six points of territory. There is a kind of diagonal break between the two stones marked ⬜, but that is all right. The territory is surrounded because there is no route leading out of it along the lines on the board that does not run into a white stone.

What about the lower left corner? This is Black's territory, but there is the white stone ⊘ left stranded within it. As was said before, there is no saving that stone, and according to the rules of go Black need not actually capture it by playing inside his own territory at 'c'. When the game is over he just takes it from the board as his prisoner, leaving himself seven vacant points here.

Again there is a diagonal break between the two stones marked ⦿, and again that is all right.

The rules of go also state that one point is to be subtracted from a player's territory for every stone lost, so we have to figure another point for White ⬠. Instead of subtracting one point from White's score for this stone, it is easier to add a point to Black's territory, so we shall follow that course and count eight points for Black in the lower left corner: six vacant points, one that becomes vacant when White ⬠ is removed, and one more "prisoner point". That is, Black gets two points for ⬠.

In the upper left corner White has surrounded ten vacant points, but on two of them, the two marked ×, black stones have been captured. As before, we shall add the two points for them to White's territory here instead of subtracting them from Black's, making White's total in this corner twelve.

The score is thus:

Black		White	
Upper right	9 points	Lower right	6 points
Lower left	8 points	Upper left	12 points
	17 points		18 points

White has won by one point.

What about the vacant point in the center of the upper edge? This is a neutral point, a sort of no-man's-land between the black and white lines, and as such it counts for neither player.

The method of counting we have just described is the natural one and is used by good players to count the territories during the course of an actual game. However, it gives too much opportunity to human error to be entirely trustworthy, so when a game is played out to the end, the players use the following foolproof procedure:

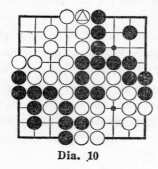

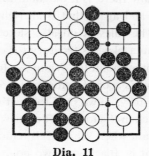

Dia. 10   Dia. 11

Step 1 (Dia. 10) The neutral points are filled in. It does not matter who fills them, and the players need not take turns here. In **Dia. 10** White has filled the only neutral point at ⊘.

Step 2 (Dia. 11) The stranded stones are removed from the board. In this game there was only one such stone, the white one in the lower left corner, and Black removes it.

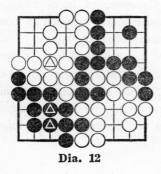

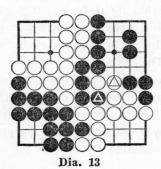

Dia. 12   Dia. 13

Step 3 (Dia. 12) The captured stones are now replaced on the board, white captives within White's territory and black captives within Black's, thus reducing each player's territory by one point for every stone he has lost. In this game White has lost one stone, which has been replaced at ⊘, and Black has lost two, which have been replaced at ▲.

Step 4 (Dia. 13) The territories are rearranged into easily countable shapes. When this has been done as shown, the score becomes:

Black	White
10+4=14 points	9+6=15 points

The totals are different from before because now points are being subtracted for prisoners instead of being added, but the margin of victory is the same. White is one point ahead.

In the process of rearrangement Black's wall has been spoiled at ⊘. This is a matter of no importance, but it could easily be tidied up by switching ⊘ and ▲.

Now you know how to play go—almost.

CHAPTER 3: CAPTURE

In this chapter we shall finish with the rules of go by explaining thoroughly how stones are captured. You will also learn how groups of stones are constructed which are safe from capture.

LIBERTIES

A single stone sitting in the middle of the board, like the one in **Dia. 1,** may be compared to a man standing at an intersection in a big city. That man can see down only four streets to just four adjacent intersections, which correspond to the points marked × in **Dia. 2.** If he is a fugitive from justice on whom the police are advancing, he remains at large so long as at least one of those intersections is open, but when the police block all four of them he is captured. Likewise the black stone in **Dia. 2** is captured and taken off the board if White gets a stone on each of the four points marked ×. The result of this capture is shown in **Dia. 3.**

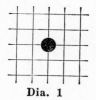

Dia. 1

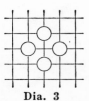

Dia. 2

Dia. 3

The four points marked × in **Dia. 2** are called the liberties of the stone there. A stone perched on the edge of the board has three liberties and a stone sitting in the corner has only two liberties, as can be seen in **Dia. 4,** so it takes three stones to capture a stone on the edge and two stones to capture one in the corner.

Enemy stones must occupy all the adjacent intersections before a stone is captured and removed. The black stone in **Dia. 5** may have a dim future, yet it has one liberty left and can stay on the board until the end of the game. At that time, provided that the surrounding white stones have survived, it will be taken from the board as a prisoner in **step 2** of the counting procedure.

So much for the capture of isolated stones. Whole groups can also be captured, as you will learn in the next section of this chapter.

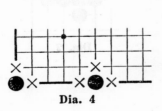

Dia. 4

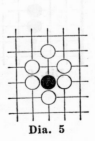

Dia. 5

SOLIDLY CONNECTED STONES

A solidly connected group of stones is one which is all joined together by direct connections along the black lines. For example, the two black stones in **Dia. 6** are solidly connected. So are the seven ones in **Dia. 7**. The two stones in **Dia. 8,** however, are not solidly connected because there is no black line running directly from one to the other. The six stones in **Dia. 9** are divided into two solidly connected groups of three stones each, separated by a diagonal break between the two stones marked ▲.

Dia. 6

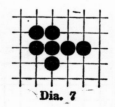

Dia. 7

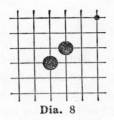

Dia. 8

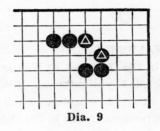

Dia. 9

For the purpose of being captured a solidly connected group acts as a single unit. The two black stones in **Dia. 6** have six liberties, which have been marked with ×'s in **Dia. 10,** and they are captured together when White gets stones on those six points. This is what happened in **Dia. 6** of chapter 2, you may recall. The solidly connected group in **Dia. 7** has eleven liberties, (count them for yourself), and is captured when and if those eleven points are occupied by White. Solidly connected stones cannot be captured one by one.

Dia. 10

EXAMPLE 1

In **Dia. 11** Black ⬣ is in atari, three of its four liberties being occupied by white stones. If White takes its last liberty by playing 1 in **Dia. 12** he captures it and removes it from the board, leaving the position shown in **Dia. 13.** Playing 1 and removing the black stone constitutes one move by White, although we have used two diagrams to show it.

This is a case, by the way, in which the capture of one stone has a big effect. Backed up by his strong, beautiful position in **Dia. 13,** White can play on the lower side of the board with impunity and can easily make territory on the left side. Compare this with **Dia. 14,** where Black has rescued his stone by playing 1. Now White ⬡ is cut off and forlorn, and the rest of the white stones are not all that strong either, so Black has a good chance to take a large territory on the lower side while holding White to a small territory on the left.

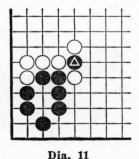

Dia. 11

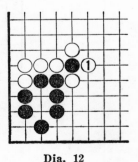

Dia. 12

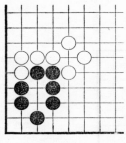

Dia. 13

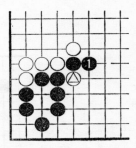

Dia. 14

EXAMPLE 2

The five white stones in **Dia. 15** are in atari, their only liberty being the corner point. If Black takes this point by playing 1 in **Dia. 16** he removes them from the board, leaving the position shown in **Dia. 17**.

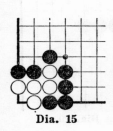

Dia. 15

Dia. 16

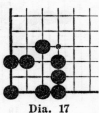

Dia. 17

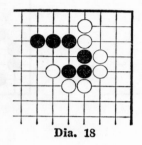

Dia. 18

EXAMPLE 3

Three of the black stones in **Dia. 18** are in atari—do you see the ones we mean? White 1 in **Dia. 19** captures them, and the position left behind is shown in **Dia. 20**.

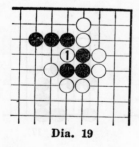

Dia. 19

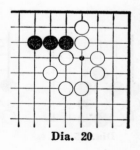

Dia. 20

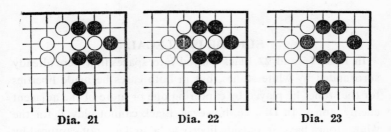

Dia. 21   Dia. 22   Dia. 23

EXAMPLE 4

This is an example of capture and recapture. White in **Dia. 21** has two stones nestled in the embrace of five black ones, and Black can take them by playing 1 in **Dia. 22**. The capturing stone, however, is itself left in atari, as you can see in **Dia. 23**. White may remove it by playing 2 in **Dia. 24**. The final result of this exchange is shown in **Dia. 25**.

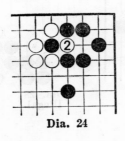

Dia. 24

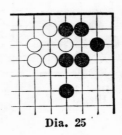

Dia. 25

SUICIDE IS ILLEGAL

In **Dias. 16** and **22** Black played into spaces that were already surrounded by white stones, but in both cases he made liberties for the stones he played by capturing one or more of the adjacent enemy stones. In **Dia. 26,** however, Black cannot play 1, for the white stones have an outside liberty at 'a' and are not captured by this move. If Black foolishly tries to play at 1, White will point out that this stone is now sitting on the board without any liberties, which is impossible under the rules of go. If Black wants to remove the white stones from the board, he must first play at 'a' to put them in atari and then play 1.

Similarly Black 1 in **Dia. 27** is illegal because it fails to capture any white stones.

White 1 in **Dia. 28** is also illegal, for it creates a three-stone group which has no liberties.

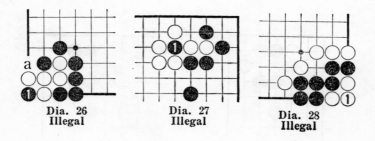

Dia. 26
Illegal

Dia. 27
Illegal

Dia. 28
Illegal

KO

Take a look at **Dia. 29.** Black ⬣ is in atari, and White can capture it by playing 1 in **Dia. 30.** White 1 itself is left in atari, so you might think that Black could recapture it by playing 2 in **Dia. 31,** restoring the position to its original state. Then White would recapture again, then Black would recapture, and so on ad infinitum. If there were no rule to govern this kind of situation, which is called ko, many games of go would end in frustration.

The rule is that when one player captures in a ko his opponent cannot immediately recapture, but must first play at least once elsewhere. That is, after White 1 in **Dia. 30** Black cannot play 2 in **Dia. 31,** but must find some other move. This position was taken from a real game, so let us follow the action and see how a ko fight goes.

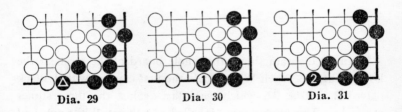

Dia. 29   Dia. 30   Dia. 31

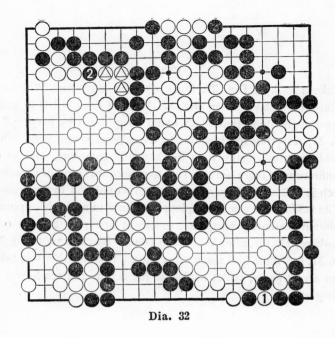

Dia. 32

The next diagram shows the whole board at the moment the ko fight began. When White made the first capture with 1 Black played 2 in **Dia. 32,** which was atari against the three stones marked △. This kind of move is called a ko threat. White now had

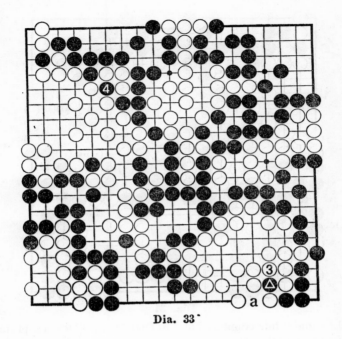

Dia. 33

the opportunity to secure four points of profit by playing 3 in **Dia. 33,** two points for capturing ⬢ and two points for having captured a stone on 'a', but then Black would earn six points by capturing three stones with 4, obviously a bad exchange for White. Therefore

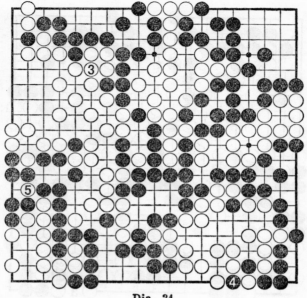

Dia. 34

in the game White connected at 3 in **Dia. 34** and Black recaptured in the ko at 4. Now it was White who had to find a ko threat, and he played 5. If Black used 6 to finish the ko by connecting as in **Dia. 35,** White 7 would capture three stones, so Black defended by capturing with 6 in **Dia. 36,** and the ko fight continued as shown. Both Black 8 and White 11 were ko threats which had to be answered, but when White captured in the ko with 13 Black made a non-compelling ko threat at 14. White finished the ko with 15, and Black played 16, which prevented White from capturing there to start a second ko. Instead of playing 14, Black could have played one of the points marked 'b' and forced White to answer, but he realized that White had more ko threats, (the points marked 'w'), than he did, and he made just as much profit with 14 and 16 as White did with 13 and 15.

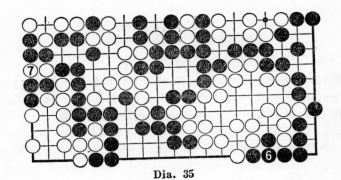

Dia. 35

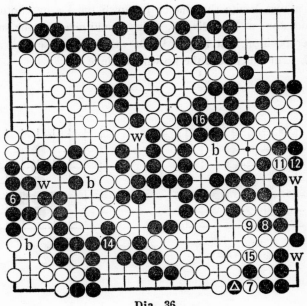

Dia. 36
10 at ⟨△⟩
⑬ at ⑦

Ko fights come in many sizes and forms, and almost every game of go has at least one of them. Here are two more examples.

In **Dia. 37** White answers Black 1 by making a ko shape, and Black 3 is the first ko capture. White must make a ko threat with 4, and Black has the chance to connect with 5 in **Dia. 38,** securing a large, strong corner and leaving the white stones helplessly weak. But if Black has to answer the ko threat, White can recapture with 6 in **Dia. 39,** and now Black must play 7 elsewhere. This allows White the chance to finish the ko by capturing a second stone at 8 in **Dia. 40,** which would give him the superior corner position, but maybe White will have to use 8 to answer Black 7, in which case the ko will continue.

Dia. 37
④ elsewhere

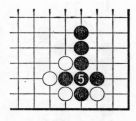

Dia. 38

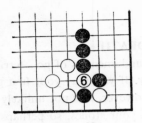

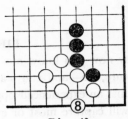

Dia. 39

Dia. 40

⑤ answers ④, elsewhere
⑦ elsewhere

Dia. 41 shows a ko shape in the corner. This ko fight is a little different from the previous two. If Black ignores the ko threat that White makes with 3, he can capture the white stones lined up on the lower edge by playing 'b', but what if he answers White 3, allowing White to recapture with 5 in **Dia. 42**? The best White can do, if he ignores Black 6, is to play atari at 7, but then Black can recapture at 'a' and the ko goes on. Later, if White recaptures at 5 and ignores a second Black ko threat, he can capture all the black stones by playing at 'b'. This ko fight favors Black in that he can win it by ignoring only one ko threat, whereas White must ignore two.

By the way, the exchange shown previously in **Dias. 21-25** was not a ko. White was allowed to play 2 immediately after Black 1 because there was no further recapturing possible, and so no chance for an infinite progression.

Dia. 41

③ elsewhere
④ answers ③

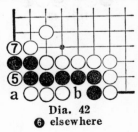

Dia. 42

⑥ elsewhere

LIFE AND DEATH

By now you know most of the fundamentals of go—territory, capture, ko—and can start to play. If you play your first game against an experienced opponent, however, it is not unlikely that he will capture most or even all of your stones, so perhaps you had better read this section, in which you will learn how to build groups of stones which are safe from capture.

Dia. 43 shows one such group. White's stones have been completely surrounded from the outside, but they possess two separated, internal liberties and are safe. Black cannot capture by playing into either one of the two liberties because the other liberty always remains open. Internal liberties are called eyes. The most basic principle of go is that groups with two or more eyes are safe, and others are not.

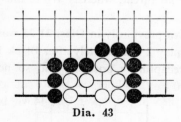

Dia. 43

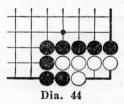

Dia. 44

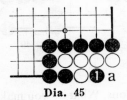

Dia. 45

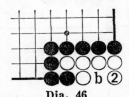

Dia. 46

Dia. 44 shows a white group which has two internal liberties, but they are not separated. This group does not have two eyes; it just has one big eye and is dead. Do you see that it can be captured? If not, look at **Dia. 45.** Black 1 puts the entire white group in atari, and next Black can capture the five white stones by taking their last liberty at 'a'. If White plays 'a' himself to capture Black 1, he is left with six stones with only one liberty, as you can see in **Dia. 46.** Black can capture all of them by playing back into 'b'.

Black should be in no hurry to play 1 in **Dia. 45,** unless his own stones on the outside begin to run short of liberties. White cannot get away. At the end of the game the white stones in **Dia. 44** will be removed from the board as prisoners without Black's actually having to occupy their last two liberties at all, just as the isolated white stone in the lower left corner of the game in chapter 2 was removed. If Black plays 1 in **Dia. 45** unnecessarily he is wasting his turn, and furthermore losing one point by filling in his own territory.

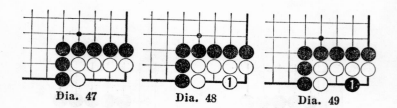

Dia. 47   Dia. 48   Dia. 49

Let us look at two more simple positions. What do you make of the white stones in **Dia. 47**? If it is White's turn, he can get two eyes by playing 1 in **Dia. 48**, giving his stones life. But if it is Black's turn and he plays 1 in **Dia. 49**, White dies. It is not hard to see that after Black 1 it is impossible for White to get two eyes, and in fact he is just two moves away from being captured. Although Black would not normally have to make those two moves, we can suppose for the sake of illustration that there are white stones on the outside as in **Dia. 50**, and Black has to capture to protect his own group. White now answers Black 1 with 2, and Black plays atari at 3. If White fills another of Black's outside liberties, Black can play at 'c' to capture the white stones in the corner. If White plays 'c', capturing Black 1 and 3, Black can play back into one of these points and White will still be left with only one liberty.

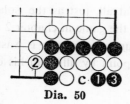

Dia. 50

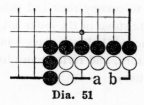

Dia. 51

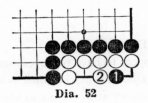

Dia. 52

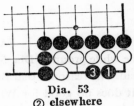

Dia. 53
② elsewhere

The white stones in **Dia. 51** are alive, because White can make two eyes by playing either 'a' or 'b'. If Black attacks with 1 in **Dia. 52,** White will answer at 2 and there is nothing more that Black can do. White 2 is necessary, for if Black gets the chance to play 3 in **Dia. 53,** the white stones die. How Black actually captures them after **Dia. 53**, should that be necessary, is shown in **Dias. 54** and **55.**

You should keep in mind that it is a waste of time actually to capture a dead group unless it becomes necesary to do so in order to protect your own stones. At the end of the game all groups which cannot form two eyes, and therefore can in theory be captured, are removed as prisoners anyway. On the other hand, dead stones must be reckoned with as long as they remain on the board, and in the complicated give and take of go it sometimes even happens that what appeared to be dead stones suddenly spring to life and help to capture the very stones which had been surrounding them.

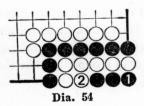

Dia. 54

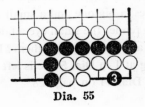

Dia. 55

FALSE EYES

The white group in **Dia. 56** may appear to have two eyes, but it is dead. The reason is that Black 1 in **Dia. 57** is atari against White ⊘. It does no good for White to connect at 3, since this would leave his whole group with only one liberty, but when Black captures at 3 White's second "eye" has disappeared and his four stones are in atari. Of course White can fight ko back and forth at 3 and ⊘, but this is no more than a delaying action and is significant only if the black stones on the outside are on the verge of being captured. White cannot connect the ko, and there is no way for him to make a second eye.

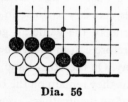

Dia. 56

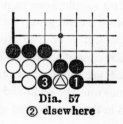

Dia. 57
② elsewhere

The right hand eye in **Dia. 56** is what is called a false eye. **Dia. 58** gives a second example. The black stones may seem to have two eyes, a big one and a small one, but the two white stones marked ⊘ render the small eye a false one. Three black stones are already in atari—do you see them? If Black tries to save them by connecting at 1 in **Dia. 59** he is left with a dead group much like the one in **Dia. 44** on page 28.

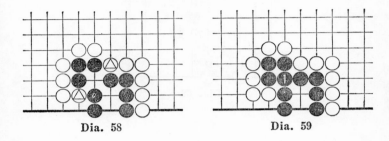

Dia. 58

Dia. 59

Dia. 60 shows a third kind of false eye. Black can count on getting one good eye at 'a', but he has no eye in the center. White 1 in **Dia. 61** puts the five black stones marked ⬤ into atari, and although Black can connect them at 2, this fills in the "eye" and leaves the whole group dead. The black groups in both **Dias. 60** and **58** and the white one in **Dia. 56** are dead as they stand.

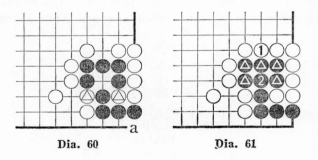

Dia. 60

Dia. 61

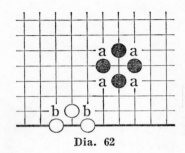

Dia. 62

It may help you to understand the difference between real eyes and false eyes if we add this explanation to our examples. In **Dia. 62** the four black stones have an eye shape, but the eye will become real only if Black controls three of the four points marked 'a'. Look back to **Dias. 58** and **60** and you will see that in both cases white stones occupy two of the 'a' points around the false eye. The three white stones in **Dia. 62** have an eye shape on the side, but to make this a real eye White must control both of the points marked 'b'. Look back to **Dia. 56** and notice the black stone on one of the 'b' points creating the false eye. In **Dia. 63** Black ⬤ makes the eyes at 'p' and 'q' both false, and White is dead. In

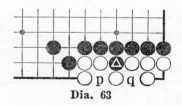

Dia. 63

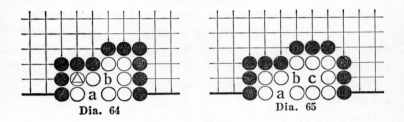

Dia. 64   **Dia. 65**

Dia. 64 the eye at 'a' is real, for White has 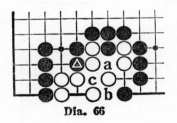 and Black cannot play 'b'. The point 'a' in **Dia. 65** is also a real eye. This time Black can play a stone at 'b', but White will capture it by playing 'c'. The groups in **Dias. 64** and **65** are alive. The group in **Dia. 66** is dead. Black already has ● and can play either 'a' or 'b' to render 'c' a false eye.

Dia. 66

EXAMPLES

Now here are some further examples. Test your understanding of what you have learned so far by working them out by yourself before looking at the answers, which appear on pages 38 and 39.

EXAMPLE 1

How can Black kill the white stones?

EXAMPLE 2

How can Black make his group alive?

EXAMPLE 3

Is White alive or can Black capture him?

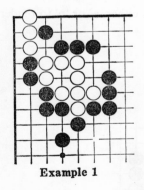

Example 1

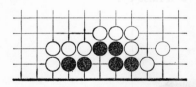

Example 2

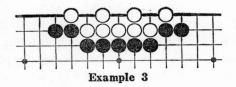

Example 3

EXAMPLE 4
White to play and kill the black stones.
EXAMPLE 5
Black to play and live.

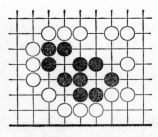

Example 4

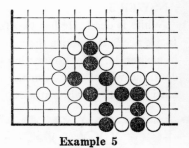

Example 5

ANSWER 1

Black 1 cuts White into two one-eyed groups, both of which are dead.

ANSWER 2

Black 1 is the move which does the trick. It forms one definite eye in the center, and a second one can be made by playing either 'a' or 'b'. If White plays 2 at 'a' Black will play 3 at 'b', or vice versa.

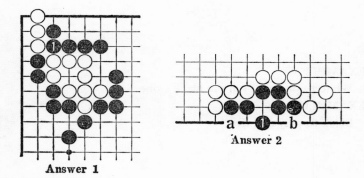

Answer 1

Answer 2

ANSWER 3

White is dead. He has two false eyes, but only one real one. If Black needs to remove the white stones he can start with 1 and 3 in **answer 3a**. After connecting this ko at ⬢ in **answer 3b**, he can continue with 1 and 3 on the other side. This second Black 3 is atari against the white stones.

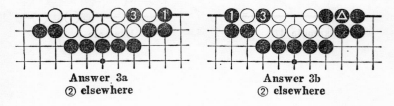

Answer 3a
② elsewhere

Answer 3b
② elsewhere

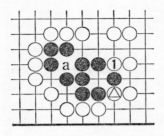

Answer 4

ANSWER 4

White 1, in conjunction with ◎, creates a false eye, and Black is dead. He has one real eye at 'a' but cannot possibly form a second one.

ANSWER 5

Black 1 in **answer 5a** is the only move. The eye at 'a' is false, but Black has two other good ones and is alive. If Black lets White play 1 in **answer 5b**, then he is left with only one real eye and is dead.

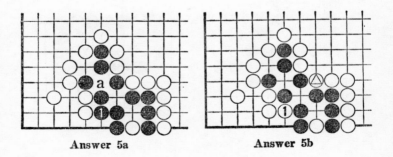

Answer 5a   Answer 5b

SEKI

We have been showing you at great length that two-eyed groups live while one-eyed or no-eyed groups die, but you will probably not be surprised to hear that there is an exception to this rule. Look at Dia. 67, for example. The two black stones marked ▲ are cut off and have not even one eye, but they cannot be captured. They share two liberties with six white stones which are similarly cut off, and neither player can occupy either one of these two points without putting his own stones into atari. Such an impasse situation is called a seki. The black and white stones are all alive, and the two points between them are not territory for either player.

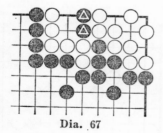

Dia. 67

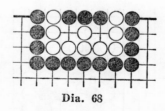

Dia. 68

Dia. 68 is another example of seki. Obviously White cannot play on either of the two internal liberties. What if Black does so, playing 1 in **Dia. 69**? White will capture four stones with 2, leaving the position shown in **Dia. 70**. He is alive because he can get two eyes by playing either 'a' or 'b'. Black 1 in **Dia. 69** is a mistake, because it gives White eight points: four points of territory and four prisoners. Black should leave the position as seki.

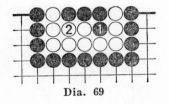

Dia. 69

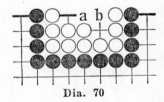

Dia. 70

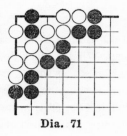

Dia. 71

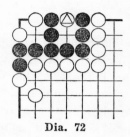

Dia. 72

Dias. **71**, **72**, **73** and **74** show other examples of seki for you to look at. In all of them stones with no eyes, or only one eye, are alive. Notwithstanding all of these examples, seki is not very common, cropping up perhaps once in twenty games.

According to the rules of go neither player can count any territory in a seki. White does not get two points in **Dia. 74,** for instance. Admittedly, this rule is somewhat arbitrary. In **Dia. 72,** by the way, Black is allowed to gain one prisoner by capturing White ⊘.

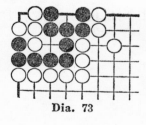

Dia. 73

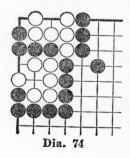

Dia. 74

Now here are two more examples for you to work out for your-self. (Answers are on the following page.)

EXAMPLE 6

This position is like **Dia. 68** except that White now has lots of liberties on the outside. Is it still seki, or can White capture the black stones?

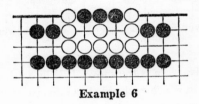

Example 6

EXAMPLE 7

Black has invaded White's corner at 1 and White has replied with 2. How should Black continue to produce a seki? (Slightly difficult.)

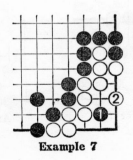

Example 7

ANSWER 6

It is still seki. White must not play 1 in **answer 6a**, for after he captures the three black stones with 3, Black 4 in **answer 6b** kills him. We studied this on page 30.

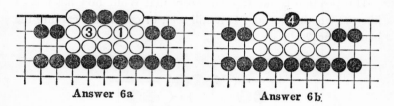

Answer 6a   Answer 6b

ANSWER 7

Black 1 in **answer 7a** is the move. If White answers at 2, Black 3 creates a seki in which each side has one eye. If White plays 2 in **answer 7b**, then Black 3 makes a seki like the one in **Dia. 71**. Black 1 in **answer 7c** does not work, for after White 2 the two black stones are left dead within White's territory.

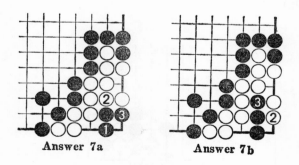

Answer 7a   Answer 7b

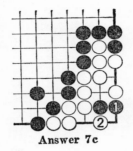

Answer 7c

These then are the basics of go. There are some more rules covering special situations which you have not met, but you will play the game for a long, long time before you run into any of them. For your reference, all the rules of go, (well, almost all of them), are summarized in the appendix at the end of the book.

PART

II

Elementary Tactics and Strategy

CHAPTER 4: AT THE EDGE OF THE BOARD

You will remember the moves in **Dia. 1** from the game in chapter 2. That game ended in a flurry of such plays at the edge of the board, which is typical of go. These plays are usually too small to be worth making in the early or middle part of the game, but they become important toward the end and mistakes in handling them can have serious consequences. They are not difficult, and make a good starting point for part II of this book. The following examples should show you what to look for when defending your territory or reducing your opponent's territory at the edge of the board.

EXAMPLE 1

What happens if White forgets to play 4 in **Dia. 1**? Black can cut at 1 in **Dia. 2**, which is atari against White △, and if White tries to run away with 2, 4, and 6 his stones will be chased into the corner, where they will meet with disaster. Black 7 takes their last liberty. Instead of playing 2 etc., it would be better for White to do nothing at all, or if anything to play as in **Dia. 3**. You must be aware of dangers like this.

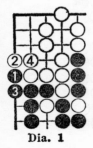
Dia. 1

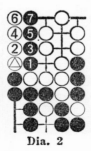
Dia. 2

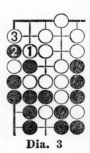
Dia. 3

EXAMPLE 2

It is not always necessary, however, to make connections like White 4 in **Dia. 1**. In **Dia. 4** White would be wasting a move, and diminishing his territory by one point, if he connected at 'a'. Black can cut with 1 in **Dia. 5**, but this time White has a strong wall of his own stones nearby, and Black cannot capture anything. For White to play 'a' in **Dia. 4** could be just as bad a mistake, if not worse, then for him not to play 4 in **Dia. 1**.

We digress here to point out that Black's abortive invasion in **Dia. 5** does not alter the score of the game. On the one hand Black has caused White to play three stones inside his own territory, reducing it by three points. On the other hand Black 1, 3 and 5 are dead, and at the end of the game they will be lifted from the board and set down again inside Black's territory, reducing it by three points. The net result is even. Black should not, however, play moves like 1, 3 and 5 just to see if his opponent is awake enough to answer correctly. He should save them for use as ko threats.

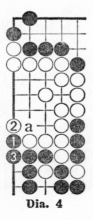

Dia. 4

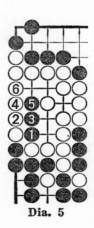

Dia. 5

We digress further to mention a significant difference between **Dias. 1** and **4**. Black 1 and 3 in **Dia. 1** are more valuable than 1 and 3 in **Dia. 4**, for two reasons. The first is that the former reduce White's territory by two points, indenting it at 2 and 4, whereas the latter reduce White's territory by only one point. The second reason is that after **Dia. 1** it is Black's turn again, whereas after **Dia. 4** it is White's turn. There are technical terms for this which you might as well learn. Black 1 and 3 in **Dia. 1** are called sente plays, meaning that White cannot afford not to answer them. (Of course they would not be sente if made too early, but toward the end of the game White's connection at 4 will probably be more important than anything else on the board, and at that time Black can play 1 and 3 in sente.)

Black 3 in **Dia. 4** is called a gote play, meaning that it need not be answered. We also say that after **Dia. 4** White has sente, meaning that it is his turn and he is free to move in some other part of the board. Sente and gote are important in go. It is often correct to make a small sente play before making a large gote one.

EXAMPLE 3

Dia. 6 shows a position in which Black 4 is very important, for if Black omits this connection he leaves himself open to the cut at White 1 in **Dia. 7**. Black 2 in **Dia. 7** is foolish. White 3 is atari against Black's two stones ⓐ, and if Black saves them by playing 4 then White 5 is atari against ⓑ. As you should be able to see, Black ⓑ cannot escape capture and White has made a big breakthrough.

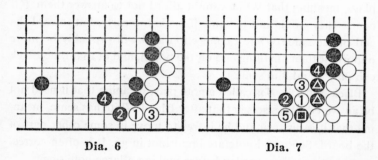

Dia. 6   Dia. 7

Black 2 in **Dia. 7** was particularly inept, but there may be no good way to deal with White 1. If Black plays 2 and 4 in **Dia. 8** he might be able to get some territory in the center, but at the cost of a big loss on the lower side. Black 2 in **Dia. 9** is the strongest resistance he can make, but White can play 3 and put up a good fight. After White 11 the Black group including 4 and 10 is cut off and may get into trouble, and Black has little chance of making territory in the center.

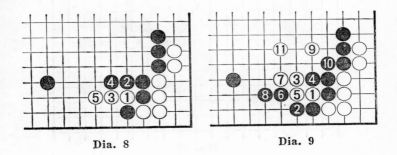

Dia. 8

Dia. 9

Black 4 in **Dia. 6** was the right way to connect, and Black 1 in **Dia. 10** is wrong. For one thing, there is more space between Black ⬤ and the black wall in **Dia. 10** than there was in **Dia. 6**, making it easier for White to invade, and for another thing Black 4 in **Dia. 6** begins to make shape for eyes while Black 1 in **Dia. 10** does not.

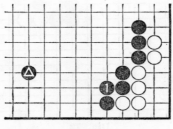

Dia. 10

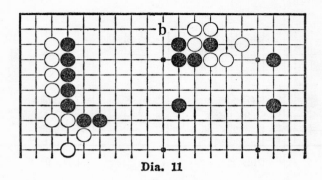

Dia. 11

EXAMPLE 4

How much territory can Black expect in the upper left center in **Dia. 11**? This area seems to be six lines wide and about seven lines high, so you might think it should amount to some forty points, but White can reduce it to half that by jumping out to 'b'. **Dia. 12** shows this. After exchanging 2 for 3 Black might, in

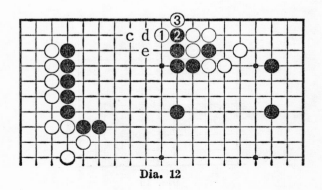

Dia. 12

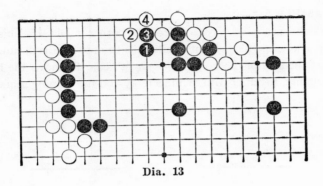

Dia. 13

various circumstances, play 'c', 'd' or 'e', or nothing further at all. In the present situation 'e' is best, defending the center, but after **Dia. 13** it is hard to imagine Black's getting much more than twenty points here. Black 1 in **Dia. 14,** or White 1 in **Dia. 12,** is a substantial middle-game play.

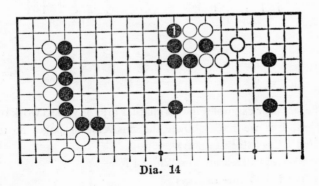

Dia. 14

EXAMPLE 5

Black 1 is a good way to defend the corner in **Dia. 15.** This is a large end-game play, for if White fails to answer, Black can slide down the side of the board to 'f' or 'g'. **Dia. 16** shows the latter possibility, together with White's reply and the ensuing sequence.

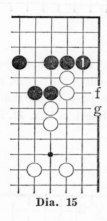

Dia. 15

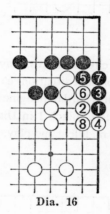

Dia. 16

The last four examples in this chapter are for you to work out by yourself, but we have shown the answers on pages 56 to 58.

EXAMPLE 6 (Black to play)

How should Black answer White 1?

EXAMPLE 7 (White to play)

There is a way for White to take away a substantial amount of Black's territory here. See if you can find it.

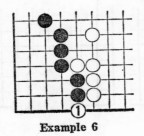

Example 6

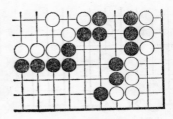

Example 7

EXAMPLE 8 (White to play)

After Black 3 White must defend against the cut at 'a'. How should he do so so as to assure himself of at least ten points of territory?

EXAMPLE 9 (White to play)

This time Black has started from the other side. Again how should White play 4 so as to get at least ten points of territory?

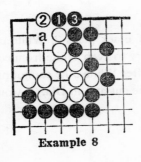

Example 8

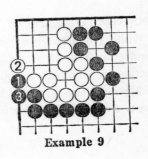

Example 9

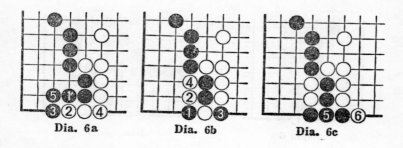

Dia. 6a   Dia. 6b   Dia. 6c

ANSWER TO EXAMPLE 6

Black should play 1 in **Dia. 6a.** If he plays 1 in **Dia. 6b,** White can cut at 2, and if Black compounds his error by capturing at 3 White 4 is atari against two stones. When Black connects at 5 in **Dia. 6c,** White 6 assures the capture of five stones.

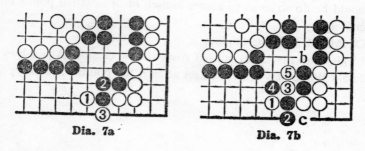

Dia. 7a   Dia. 7b

ANSWER TO EXAMPLE 7

White 1 in **Dia. 7a** is the move. If Black plays 2, White can connect underneath at 3. Black may try to keep White from connecting by playing 2 in **Dia. 7b,** but after White 5 he cannot prevent both White 'b' and White 'c'. The cut at 1 in **Dia. 7c** would just not work in this situation.

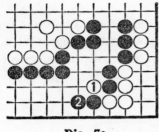

Dia. 7c

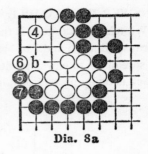

Dia. 8a

ANSWER TO EXAMPLE 8

White should play 4 in **Dia. 8a**. Then if Black plays 5 and 7, White need not protect against the threat of Black 'b', a cut which would fail because of the placement of White 4, but can take sente elsewhere with ten points of territory left in the corner. If White mistakenly plays 4 in **Dia. 8b**, Black can play 5 and 7 in sente and reduce the corner to nine points.

When White plays 4 correctly he may even get eleven points, because Black may well not want to play 5 and 7 in **Dia. 8a** in gote, and White may later play 1 in **Dia. 8c**.

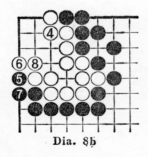

Dia. 8b

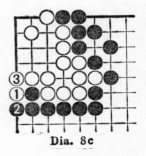

Dia. 8c

ANSWER TO EXAMPLE 9

White's correct move is the same as before, as shown in **Dia. 9**. It causes Black 5 and 7 to become gote, and once again White can be sure of ten or eleven points in the corner, depending on whether Black actually plays 5 or not.

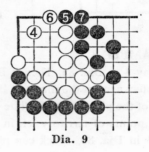

Dia. 9

CHAPTER 5: SHICHO

This is the first of a series of short chapters covering various methods for capturing stones. We hope that you will keep in mind as you read them that capturing is not the point of the game—one of the main differences between strong players and beginners is that the latter often cannot bear to give up anything and are always getting into unnecessary battles over a few unimportant stones, while the former abandon stones willingly in order to obtain territory. All the same, every go player needs to learn the basic techniques described here.

In **Dia. 1** Black plays atari against White ⬡ with 1. White runs out at 2, but Black gives atari again with 3 and 5, forcing White to flee in a zig-zag pattern. How will this end?

Continuing as in **Dia. 2**, Black drives the white stones into the edge of the board. After Black 17 they can flee no farther, and White has suffered a catastrophe. Needless to say, he should have given up ⬡ in **Dia. 1** as soon as Black played 1, instead of trying in vain to escape with 2 and the rest. This kind of zig-zag formation is called a shicho.

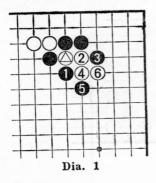

Dia. 1

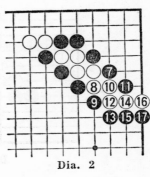

Dia. 2

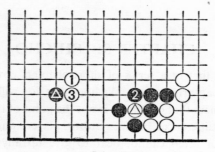

Dia. 3

What you can do when confronted with a shicho is illustrated
in **Dia. 3.** Instead of trying to run with ⊘, White plays 1. This
stone lies in the path of the shicho, and Black must capture at
2, letting White play a second stone at 3, which is rather hard on
Black ⬤. If Black answers White 1 with 2 in **Dia. 4,** then White
can escape with 3. White 13 becomes atari against Black 10,
White cannot be captured, and Black is left with some extremely
weak stones in the center. A move like White 1 is called a shicho
breaker.

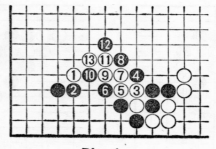

Dia. 4

Occasionally we find a beginner tracing the path of a shicho with his finger to determine whether it will work, like the one in **Dias. 1** and **2**, or is broken, like the one in **Dia. 4**. However such boorish behavior is unnecessary. You can easily read out a shicho by eye alone, especially if you use the handicap points, (the dotted points on the board), as landmarks.

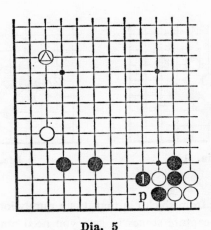

Dia. 5

For example, suppose Black is thinking of playing 1 in **Dia. 5** and wants to know if the shicho works. Well, if he plays 1 the shicho will pass through the handicap point in the middle of the lower side turning left. It will therefore also pass through the handicap point in the middle of the left side, turning left, and will run right into White △. So Black had better not play 1, but rather at 'p', or at the handicap point on the left side.

CHAPTER 6: GETA AND LOOSE SHICHO

GETA

White 1 in **Dia. 1** is an example of the technique known as geta. This play traps the two black stones marked ▲, and they cannot escape. Black may struggle for freedom as shown in **Dia. 2**, but after White 4 his stones are in atari. **Dia. 3** gives another example of geta, this time at the edge of the board.

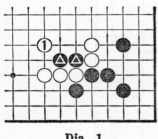

Dia. 1

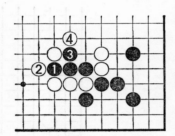

Dia. 2

Geta differs from shicho in that it is a purely local affair, that is, when you capture stones in geta you need not worry about shicho breakers appearing on the other side of the board. There are, however, moves like Black 1, 3 and 5 in **Dia. 4** which a player who has lost some stones in geta can put to use.

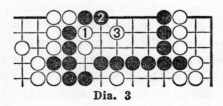

Dia. 3

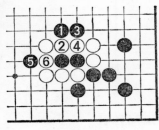

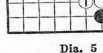

Dia. 5

Dia. 4

LOOSE SHICHO

White has played 1 in **Dia. 5**, trying to escape. Do you think he can be captured? Please cogitate for a moment before looking at the next diagram.

Black 1 to 7 in **Dia. 6** are the correct moves. At the end of this diagram the white stones have been forced to the edge of the board and have only two liberties, and their demise is inevitable. This kind of sequence is called a loose shicho. It is a bit like a real shicho, but Black's plays are not all atari.

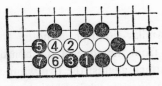

Dia. 6

CHAPTER 7: SEMEAI

Another common method of capturing stones is to drive them toward the edge of the board where they are smothered, so to speak. Here we shall look at such tactics in operation, at the battles known as semeai which they often involve, and at the business of counting liberties in these battles.

EXAMPLE 1

White 1 in **Dia. 1** is a simple example. It is atari against the stone ⬣, which Black now may as well give up for lost. He can run out at 2 in **Dia. 2**, but White follows with another atari at 3 and it is all up.

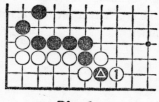

Dia. 1

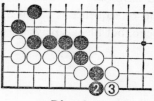

Dia. 2

EXAMPLE 2

Dia. 3 shows a similar situation, although this time the stones are a little farther from the edge of the board. Black has some chance to counterattack against the two white stones marked ◿, but they have three liberties while Black has only two, so White can capture Black before Black captures White. After this diagram,

Black may seek additional liberties by turning down at 1 in **Dia. 4,** but White blocks him at 2 and still the black stones have only two liberties while White has three. After **Dia. 3** the correct course of action is for Black to play as in **Dia. 5,** surrendering his two stones, which were doomed anyway, but getting some valuable moves in around the outside.

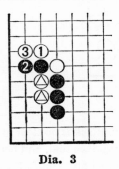

Dia. 3

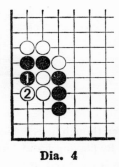

Dia. 4

Black 2 in **Dia. 3** is a good stone to play, even though it is captured in the end. If Black simply plays 2 in **Dia. 6,** he does not get to play 'a' and 'b' with sente. This trick of sacrificing two stones, as in **Dias. 3** and **5,** instead of playing 2 as in **Dia. 6,** is worth remembering.

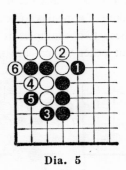

Dia. 5

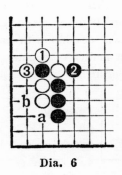

Dia. 6

EXAMPLE 3

In **Dia.** 7 there are two L-shaped groups of four stones each which are cut off and must fight it out. The black one has three liberties, while the white one has four. Suppose that it is Black's turn to play—can you see what will happen?

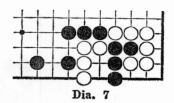

Dia. 7

Even though he is behind by one liberty, Black is not lost in this case. By playing 1 and 3 in **Dia. 8** he can produce seki, and neither group is captured. It is important for him to fill White's liberties from the outside in this way, and not try to fill from the inside as in **Dia. 9**. White 2 in **Dia. 9** is atari, and Black loses.

Dias. 3 to 9 give two simple illustrations of semeai, that is, of battles between two adjacent and opposing groups of stones, neither of which has room to form two eyes. A semeai always ends either in the capture of one of the two groups or in seki. The ability to foresee correctly the outcome of semeai is something you will develop with practice. In these two examples it was just a matter of counting liberties, but other semeai are more complicated.

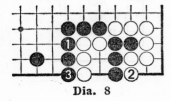

Dia. 8

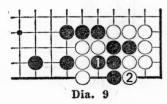

Dia. 9

Now have a go at the following examples. The answers are given on pages 68 to 71.

EXAMPLE 4 (Black to play)

White has extended out to 1. How can Black keep him from getting away?

EXAMPLE 5 (White to play)

How can White capture Black ▲? Does he have more than one move here?

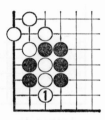

Example 4

Example 5

EXAMPLE 6 (White to play)

This is the position at move 29 in the game in chapter two, except that Black ▲ has been added. Suppose that Black plays 1. Can White capture him?

EXAMPLE 7 (Black to play)

Which is better after White 3: Black 'a' or Black 'b'? Also, what about Black 'c'? This problem is not as clear-cut as the previous ones, but see what you can figure out on your own before looking at the answer.

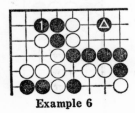

Example 6

Example 7

ANSWER 4

Black 2 in **answer 4a** is correct. After 4, White is trapped. If Black incorrectly plays 2 in **answer 4b**, White will get away by capturing the two stones marked ⬤. They have only two liberties while the white stones have three.

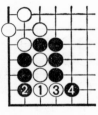

Answer 4a

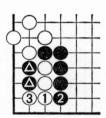

Answer 4b

ANSWER 5

White 1 in **answer 5a** is the only correct move. If White plays 1 in **answer 5b**, he will be unable to play on either side of Black 2 without putting his own stones in atari.

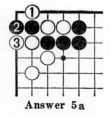

Answer 5a

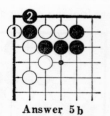

Answer 5b

ANSWER 6

In this example the three black stones and the two white ones to their right each have three liberties, so White must begin by playing 1 in **answer 6a**. Black can capture one stone with 2 and 4, but it all ends well. White 5 is atari against the original three black stones. If White plays 1 in **answer 6b**, Black will play 2 and go ahead in the fight, four liberties to three. In **answer 6b**, the white stones marked ⊘ are lost.

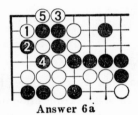

Answer 6a

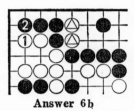

Answer 6b

ANSWER 7

To take the worst move first, Black 1 in **answer 7a** is out of the question. White turns outward at 2. If Black blocks at 3, White 4 is atari against both ▲ and ▲, and Black is in a pretty fix, but if Black runs along the third line, as in **answer 7b**, White can gain plenty of liberties and Black 1 and ▲, which have only three liberties, are left dead in the corner.

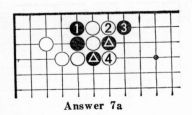

Answer 7a

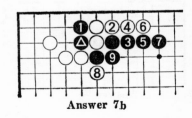

Answer 7b

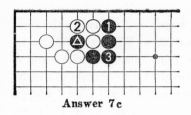

Answer 7c

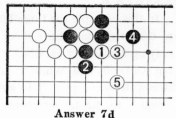

Answer 7d

Black 1 in **answer 7c** is far better. The stone ⬤ is sacrificed, but Black can get a nice wall by connecting at 3. This connection may not be absolutely necessary, but if it is omitted, White can attack as in **answer 7d,** or in some such fashion.

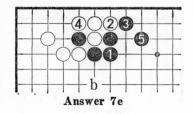

Answer 7e

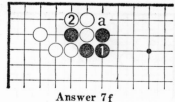

Answer 7f

But generally Black 1 in **answer 7e** is the best move. **Answer 7e** is usually better for Black than before because his stones are closer to having two eyes than in **answer 7c**. Also, instead of 5 Black might play 'b' or some other point, according to circumstances. White will probably play 2 in **answer 7f** instead of **7e**, but now Black has no cutting points to worry about and can make his next play wherever he likes—perhaps at 'a' but probably somewhere else. Of course, if White fails to answer Black 1, Black can play at 3 in **answer 7g** and now White loses his two stones.

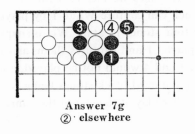

Answer 7g
② · elsewhere

CHAPTER 8: SNAP-BACK AND OIOTOSHI

SNAP-BACK

Three of the black stones in **Dia. 1** are vulnerable to capture. Do you see the ones we mean? White 1 in **Dia. 2** is atari against them. Black can capture White 1 by playing 2 in **Dia. 3**, but now he has four stones in atari. White snaps back into the point where he played 1 and captures them, as shown in **Dia. 4**. In practice **Dias. 3** and **4** would not be played, and **Dia. 2** would be left as is, the three dead black stones being removed from the board without further play at the end of the game.

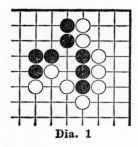

Dia. 1

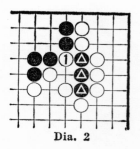

Dia. 2

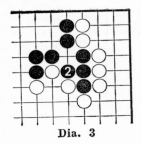

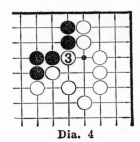

Dia. 3   Dia. 4

In **Dia. 5** White has leap-frogged into the corner with 1, and Black has unwisely tried to cut him off with 2. After Black 4 do you see the snap-back coming? What is White's next play?

White plays 5 in **Dia. 6**. Now if Black plays 'a', capturing ⬨, White will play back into the point under ⬨ and recapture three black stones. In **Dia. 5** Black should play 3 or 4 instead of 2.

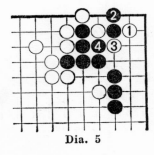

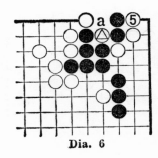

Dia. 5   Dia. 6

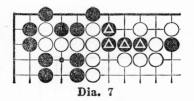

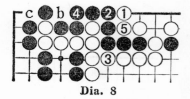

Dia. 7   Dia. 8

OIOTOSHI

In **Dia. 7** White can capture the four black stones marked ▲. In a sense these stones are connected to the strong ones on the left side, but Black must add so many stones (four) to make the connection solid that he cannot quite reach safety if White plays first. **Dia. 8** shows the sequence. After White 5 Black's stones are in atari, and if he connects at 'b' White will capture at 'c'. When White plays 1, Black should resign himself to a loss and play 'b', if anything.

This kind of capture often needs to be helped along by a sacrifice, such as Black 1 in **Dia. 9**, which prevents the formation of an eye. Black 3 is atari, but if White connects at 4 in **Dia. 10** his solid mass of stones will be thrown into atari again by Black 5 and captured.

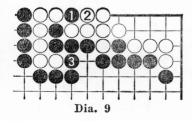

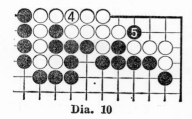

Dia. 9   Dia. 10

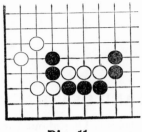
Dia. 11

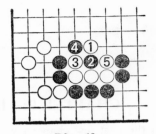
Dia. 12

The so-called cranes nest formation shown in **Dia. 11** provides a good example in the center of the board. The three white stones, (the eggs in the nest), cannot escape. If White tries to flutter out to 1 in **Dia. 12**, Black will throw in a stone at 2, and let it be captured. When he plays 6 in **Dia. 13** he puts five stones in atari, and obviously there is no point in White's connecting at 'a'.

The kind of capture seen in the last three examples is called oiotoshi. Snap-back and oiotoshi depend on the existence of, or the possibility of creating, false eyes in the stones to be captured, and once you appreciate this fact you will have no trouble anticipating them in your own games.

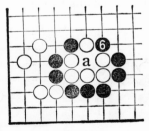
Dia. 13

CHAPTER 9: LIFE AND DEATH

In the past few chapters we have been talking about various methods of capturing small groups of stones. Now we are going to deal with the more important matter of killing large groups of stones by preventing them from forming two eyes. This topic of life and death was introduced in chapter 3, but here is a more systematic and detailed discussion.

EYE SHAPE

It often happens that a group of stones contains an empty space consisting of several points which is not divided into two eyes, and it is necessary for you to know whether such a space has the right size and shape for safety or not. For example, the two black groups in **Dia. 1** both contain three vacant points. As you will remember from chapter 3, the one on the right is not safe, and can be killed by a white stone at 'a'. In the same way White 'b' kills the group on the left. If it is Black's turn, then he can save the group on the left by playing 'b', or the one on the right by playing 'a', in either case making two eyes.

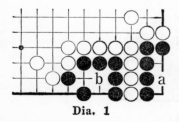

Dia. 1

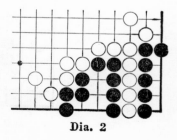

Dia. 2

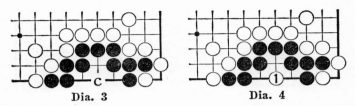

Dia. 3   Dia. 4

As you also learned in chapter 3, four in a row is alive. It does
not matter whether the four spaces are in a straight line or bent.
The two black groups in **Dia. 2**, for instance, are both alive.

There are two other shapes that can be made by four spaces,
one of which is shown in **Dia. 3**. Here 'c' is the key point. If Black
plays there he is alive with three eyes, but if White plays 1 in **Dia.
4**, Black dies. Let us see why.

Although he need not actually make these moves, White can
put the black stones into atari by playing 3 and 5 in **Dia. 5**. If
Black captures the three white intruders, White will play back
onto the point ◯ and Black cannot make two eyes.

It so happens that in this example there is another way for
Black to relieve the atari, that is by capturing a white stone with
6. This is a first capture in a ko, but instead of looking for a ko
threat White should just connect at 7, leaving what is shown in
Dia. 6. The eye at 'd' is a false one, and it does no good for Black
to capture the three white stones because White will just play back
onto ◯, so Black is really dead.

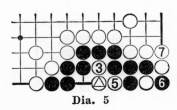

Dia. 5

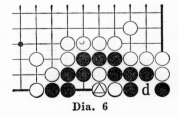

Dia. 6

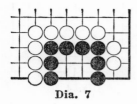

Dia. 7

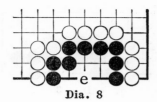

Dia. 8

The shape shown in **Dia. 7** is so bad that Black is dead even if he plays first. This is not hard to see.

Dia. 8 shows a common shape consisting of five spaces that is not safe. As you might suppose, 'e' is the key point, and if Black plays there he is alive. If White plays 1 in **Dia. 9**, however, the black stones are dead. Nothing more need be done to them, and they will be removed from the board at the end of the game, but the reason is that in theory White could play 3, 5 and 7 in **Dia. 10**, putting Black into atari. The four white stones have the same shape as was studied in **Dias. 3-6**, and if Black captures them White will play back onto ⊘.

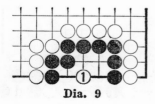

Dia. 9

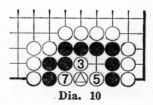

Dia. 10

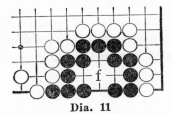

Dia. 11

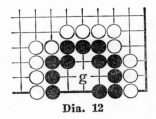

Dia. 12

The shape of five spaces shown in **Dia. 11** is much the same. If Black plays 'f' he lives, but if White plays there he dies.

There is even one shape containing six spaces that is not safe, the one in **Dia. 12**. The point 'g' is, of course, the key point, and a white stone there kills the black group. White can fill up Black's eye space with 1, 3, 5, 7 and 9 in **Dia. 13,** making the shape shown in **Dia. 8,** and if Black captures these five stones White will play again at the point 1.

The shapes of three, four, five, and six spaces shown in **Dias. 1, 3, 7, 8, 11,** and **12** are the basic ones which are not safe, and you will soon come to recognize them whenever you see them.

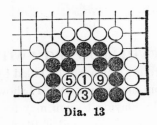

Dia. 13

THE DEATH BLOW FROM WITHIN

We have just been looking at some examples of groups which can be killed by plays striking at key points within their eye shapes. This kind of thing is so common that we would like to show you yet another example.

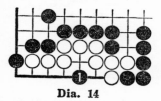
Dia. 14

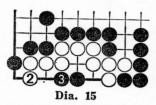
Dia. 15

Black 1 in **Dia. 14** is the only play that kills the white group there. Obviously if White were able to play 1, he would have at least two eyes. It may not be so obvious that the white group in **Dia. 14** has died, but if White tries to get eye shape by playing 2 in **Dia. 15** Black will answer with 3, and in theory he can later put White in atari with the plays marked ⬤ in **Dia. 16**. As you know by now White cannot live by capturing the four black stones in **Dia. 16**, for Black will play back into the center of this shape.

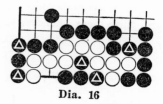
Dia. 16

THE DEATH BLOW FROM WITHOUT

There are also groups which can be killed by plays that reduce their eye shapes from the outside. **Dia. 17** shows one such group. White must begin by playing 1—you may try and see for yourself that no other play works—and if Black answers at 2 then

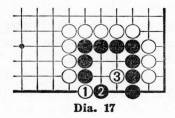

Dia. 17

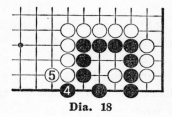

Dia. 18

White 3 kills in a familiar shape. Black can capture White 1 by playing 4 in **Dia. 18**, but by doing so he creates only a false eye, and White 5 stops his escape.

Black 1 in **Dia. 19** is an even simpler example of this technique, and once again it happens to be the only move that kills. White may answer with 2 in **Dia. 20**, but Black narrows his eye space again with 3, and finally strikes in the center of three in a row with 5. The 1-2 point in the corner, where Black played 1, is often the key point for life and death. If Black started with 1 in **Dia. 21** White could live by playing there himself, getting the live shape of four in a row.

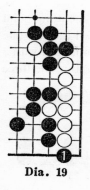

Dia. 19

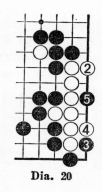

Dia. 20

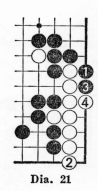

Dia. 21

CUTTING POINTS

Although the shapes listed in the first section of this chapter are the only ones which are intrinsically unsafe, cutting points can render many other ones vulnerable. The rectangular six shape illustrated in **Dia. 22,** for example, is usually perfectly secure. If Black attacks at 1 White will answer at 2, and then if Black plays 3 White will play 4, or vice versa, making two eyes. If we introduce a cutting point as in **Dia. 23**, however, the situation changes. Black ● and White's lack of outside liberties combine to make 1 a killing play, for this time White cannot answer 3 at 'h' without putting most of his own stones into atari.

White 2 in **Dia. 24** is fruitless, for it allows Black to destroy White's eye shape with 3.

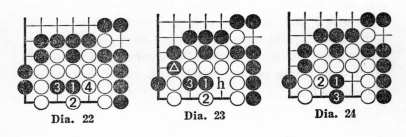

Dia. 22   Dia. 23   Dia. 24

Dia. 25 gives us a different kind of example of a cutting point used to kill a group. It is easy to see that after Black 1 there, White is dead. Black can bring half of the white stones into atari with 3 and 5 in **Dia. 26**, and although White can next capture the three

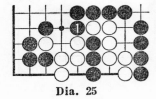

Dia. 25

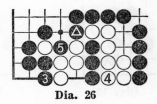

Dia. 26

black stones, this would not leave him with enough space for safety. Actually all three of the plays in **Dia. 26** are sheer wastes of time. The fight was over when Black played ⬤.

If White is able to repair the cutting point by playing 1 in **Dia. 27**, then he lives. This shape has become seki; White has no territory, but he is not dead and that is the important thing.

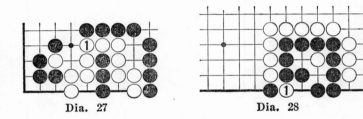

Dia. 27   Dia. 28

THROW-IN PLAYS

One of the more common ways to deprive a group of eyes is illustrated in **Dia. 28.** If Black were able to play at 1 he would have his second eye, but now that White has played there Black cannot get more than a false eye. Perhaps he will try to run out with 2 in **Dia. 29**, but White 3 neatly stops him, and 5 is atari. Although Black 6 captures the original throw-in stone, it has done its work and Black is left with no real eye on the lower edge, as you can see in **Dia. 30.**

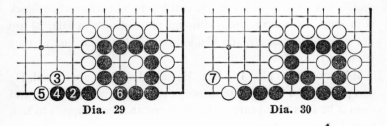

Dia. 29   Dia. 30

You can even make false eyes by sacrificing two stones, as is shown in **Dia. 31.** In that diagram White has exactly one eye on the lower edge, so Black 1 in the center becomes the key point of life and death. White can capture the two black stones by playing 2 in **Dia. 32,** but then Black throws in another stone at the key point and White can get nothing but a false eye by capturing it.

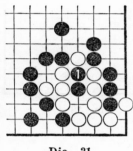

Dia. 31

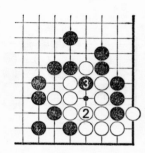

Dia. 32

ME ARI ME NASHI

This Japanese phrase means, "I have an eye and you do not," and one example of the situation it describes is shown in **Dia. 33.** White has an eye in the corner, and White 1 prevents Black from forming one. Since Black cannot afford to capture the four white stones in the shape they have, he is helpless. White can fill the outside liberties at the points marked ⊘ in **Dia. 34,** then play 1 and 3, and because of his eye he still has two liberties while Black is in atari. Of course, the additional plays shown in **Dia. 34** are not actually necessary, the black stones being dead just as they stand in **Dia. 33.**

If Black gets to play 1 in **Dia. 35,** then the tables are turned. He can pick up the three white stones in the corner at his leisure, and even if he fails to capture them the worst that can happen to him is seki.

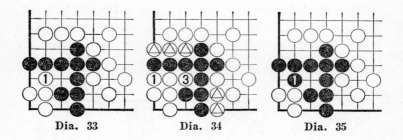

Dia. 33 Dia. 34 Dia. 35

BENT FOUR IN THE CORNER

There is one notable exception to the general rule that four in a row are alive, that is the shape shown in **Dia. 36**. Due to the peculiarities of the corner and to Black's dearth of outside liberties, White can produce a ko by attacking with 1 in **Dia. 37**. After White 3 Black must find a ko threat, and if White ignores it he can kill the black stones by connecting at 5 in **Dia. 38**.

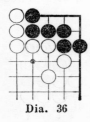

Dia. 36

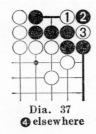

Dia. 37
❹ elsewhere

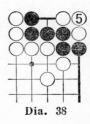

Dia. 38

When Black has two outside liberties, as in **Dia. 39**, he is safe. The attack comes as before, but now after White 3 he can play 4 in **Dia. 40**, and when he captures the two white stones he will have two eyes.

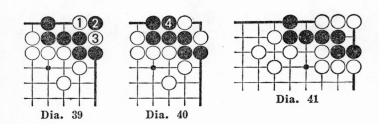

Dia. 39   Dia. 40   Dia. 41

In **Dia. 41** we have what at first appears to be seki, but in fact the black stones there are dead. The reason for this is that at the end of the game White could make some extra plays to solidify his positions, eliminating all of Black's ko threats, then attack with 1, 3 and 5 in **Dia. 42**. Black would have to capture the white stones in the bent four shape by playing 6, but then White would continue with 7 and 9 in **Dia. 43**. Since Black would have no ko threats, he would be powerless to prevent the capture of his stones. White need not actually make plays elsewhere on the board to deprive Black of ko threats. The black group in **Dia. 41** is dead just as it stands, because in principle it can be captured and Black has no way to defend it.

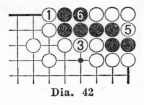

Dia. 42

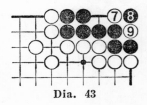

Dia. 43

FURTHER EXAMPLES

Here are some more examples illustrating various techniques of life and death. See if you can work them out for yourself before looking at the answers, which are on pages 90 to 93.

EXAMPLE 1

Black to play and kill the white group.

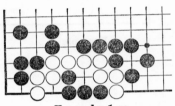

Example 1

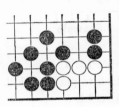

Dia. 44

The next two examples deal with the white group shown in **Dia. 44,** which is dead.

EXAMPLE 2

White has tried to live by playing ⊘. How can Black kill him?

EXAMPLE 3

This time White has tried ⊘. Black to play and kill.

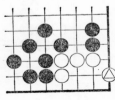

Example 2

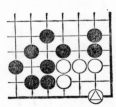

Example 3

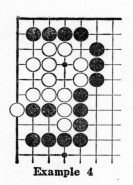

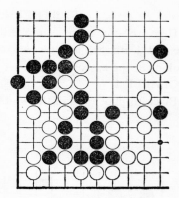

Example 4

Example 5

EXAMPLE 4

Black to play and kill.

EXAMPLE 5

Black to play and save his isolated group.

EXAMPLE 6

Black to play and live.

EXAMPLE 7

Black to play and kill.

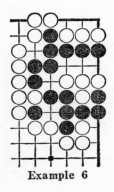

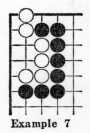

Example 7

Example 6

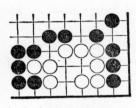

Example 8

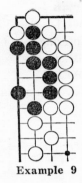

Example 9

EXAMPLE 8
Black to play and kill.

EXAMPLE 9
White to play and kill.

EXAMPLE 10
White to play. There is only one correct point for attacking this black group.

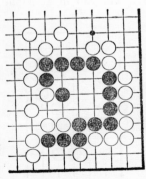

Example 10

ANSWER 1

Black 1 is the killing move. If White played there he could live by capturing four in a row, but with the shape made by Black 1, he is dead.

ANSWER 2

Black 1 is not hard to find, remembering the basic shape of **Dia. 9**.

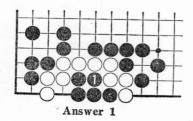

Answer 1

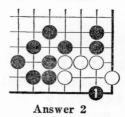

Answer 2

ANSWER 3

It is necessary to start with Black 1, for if White played there he would be alive.

ANSWER 4

Black 1 in **answer 4a** destroys White's second eye. If White blocks with 2, Black will slip in at 3 and, if White captures,

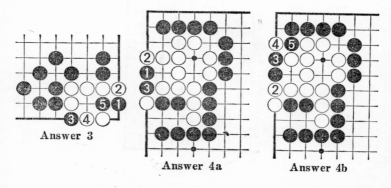

Answer 3

Answer 4a

Answer 4b

sacrifice another stone at 3 to make the eye false. If White plays 2 in **answer 4b**, then Black 3 and 5 accomplish the same thing.

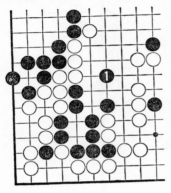

Answer 5a

Answer 5b

ANSWER 5

Black 1 in **answer 5a** is the only move which forms a second eye. You can check that there is no way for White to take this eye away. If Black plays 1 in **answer 5b**, White 2 kills him, and similarly Black 1 in **answer 5c** fails.

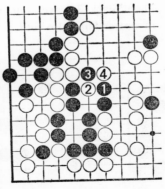

Answer 5c

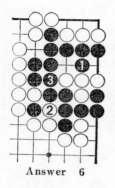

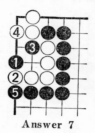

Answer 6

Answer 7

ANSWER 6

Black 1 is the key point, and after 3 Black is alive in seki. If he began by playing 3, then White at 1 would kill him.

ANSWER 7

Black 1 and 3 are the right combination. If White tries to approach with 4, Black plays 5 and White is in atari.

ANSWER 8

Black 1 in **answer 8a** is the only move that works in this case. If White plays 2, then Black 3 leaves him with only one eye. White's resistance in **answer 8b** is also futile.

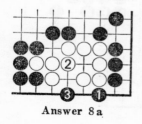

Answer 8a

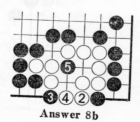

Answer 8b

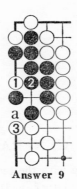

Answer 9

ANSWER 9

White 1 and 3 leave Black hopeless. Because of the presence of White 1 he cannot play at 'a', while if he captures White 1, White will play at 'a'.

ANSWER 10

White 1 in **answer 10a** is the key point—notice its relation to White ⊘. If White were to attack at 2 or 3, Black would play at 1 and live. As it is, Black must play 2 and 4, and the life of his group will depend on a ko fight. If Black plays 2 in **answer 10b**, then he dies outright.

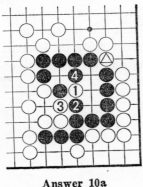

Answer 10a

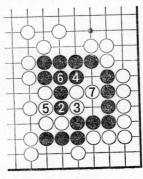

Answer 10b

CHAPTER 10:   GENERAL STRATEGY

We have finished dealing with the tactics of go, and the time has come to see about the larger questions: what to do in the opening of the game, how to develop territory, how to play over the whole board. The present chapter is devoted to such matters, and you can learn more by studying the example games in chapter 12.

THE CORNERS ARE IMPORTANT

In the first part of the game the four corners of the board have the greatest importance, and it is common to see the first few stones played in them. The reason for this is fairly obvious. If you form territory in a corner, then two of the walls are already supplied for you by the edges of the board, whereas along the side only one wall is given you and in the center you must build all four walls yourself. This means that it is in the corners that you can get the greatest amount of territory for the least number of stones played. It is also easiest to form two eyes in the corner, should you have to defend your stones.

This does not mean that you must take corner territory to win, even though there is a go saying to that effect. You cannot, however, afford to ignore the corners and allow your opponent to make large territories in all of them uncontested.

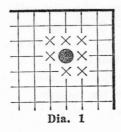

Dia. 1

It is thought best to place the first stone in an open corner on the handicap point, (the 4–4 point, which is marked with a dot), or on one of the adjacent points marked with an × in **Dia. 1**.

In many games the action starts in the corners, then extends along the sides, and only finally moves upwards into the center. This is natural, but in go there are no set ways to play in the opening. You are on your own from the first move of the game, free to try whatever schemes your imagination can invent. Often fighting will erupt from a corner or side into the center early in the game, and occasionally a battle will slowly spread from one corner to cover the whole board, like a forest fire advancing in all directions.

SHIMARI

Once you have played one stone in a corner, it is not a bad idea to add another stone to it, making what is called a shimari. **Dias. 2–4** show three of the common shimari formations, and others are possible.

A shimari does not really secure the corner territory. Of course it is a big step in that direction, and for the time being the corners in **Dias. 2–4** are Black's, but there is no telling what might happen in the fighting to come. The chief value of a shimari is that it makes a stable position from which to extend, and around which it is hard for the other player to gain a safe foothold.

Perhaps you think that it is inefficient to place two stones so close to each other early in the game, but hundreds of years of experience have proven the value of a shimari. First to establish a strong base and then to play on a larger scale is one good strategy in go.

Dia. 2

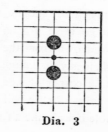

Dia. 3

Dia. 4

Black 1 in **Dia. 5** is a good shimari based on a stone on the 4–4 point. It reaches out a helping hand to Black ● and forms a loose but large territorial framework.

In **Dia. 6** Black has acquired a powerful position on the right side and a shimari such as White 1 is the ideal move to use against it. White 1 prepares for later extensions to 'a' or 'b' or such points.

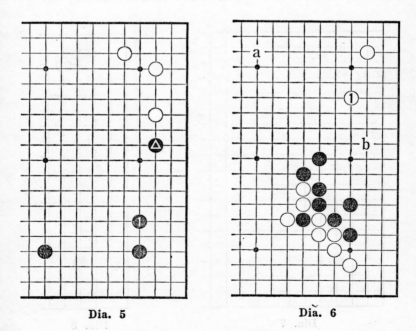

Dia. 5   Dia. 6

EXTENSIONS

This brings us to the subject of extensions, such as White 1 in **Dia. 7.** When White plays this stone he is by no means sure that the area between it and his shimari will actually end up as his territory, but at least there is the chance of that, and White has much better prospects on the left side than does Black.

When extending along the side of the board you should as a general rule play on the third or fourth line. Instead of playing White 1 in **Dia. 7,** White might prefer to play one point to its right. On the upper side White would like to extend to one of the points marked ✕, but an extension in the direction of 1 is more valuable because it is an extension from both of the shimari stones, while an extension to ✕ would be an extension from only one of

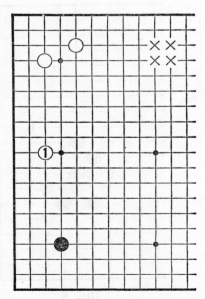

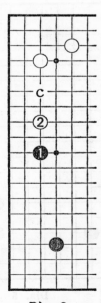

Dia. 7   Dia. 8

them. Black 1 in **Dia. 8** is also a good extension, and White 2 is a good counter-extension. If White does not play 2, then Black will be eager to extend even closer to the shimari at 'c'.

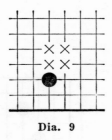

Dia. 9

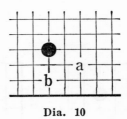

Dia. 10

When an extension is made on the third line, it is mainly vulnerable to pressure from above. In **Dia. 9** White could play one of the points marked ×, hoping to hold Black to a small territory along the edge of the board. Against an extension on the fourth line, however, it is generally better to attack from below. In **Dia. 10** White might play 'a', aiming to slip under the black stone to 'b' in the future.

White 1 in **Dia. 11** is a typical extension made for defensive purposes. Later on, if Black plays 'c', White can maintain a comfortable position by extending to 'd', or vice versa. If White extended even one line further, to 1 in **Dia. 12**, Black could invade at 2 and White, outnumbered five to two on the left side, would be in trouble. On the other hand, if White extended more narrowly, as in **Dia. 13**, he would be annoyed by Black's counterextension to 2. White 3 at 'd' would leave him with a safe position, but it would be a bit cramped as compared with **Dia. 11**. White 1 in **Dia. 11** is just right in situations like this.

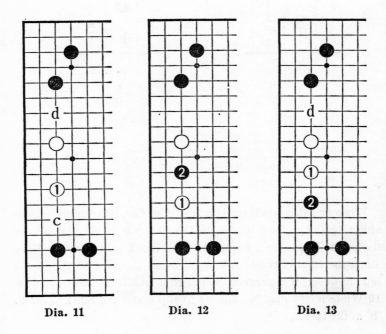

Dia. 11   Dia. 12   Dia. 13

When extending toward or in the center a one point skip, like Black 1 in **Dia. 14**, is natural and good. Next Black might skip again to 'e', 'f', or 'g', while White should probably answer Black 1 by playing 'e' himself, to defend his own position.

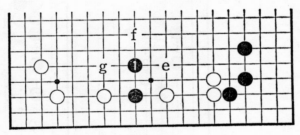

Dia. 14

White 1 in **Dia. 15** is another kind of extension often used in the center, which in this case works well to reduce Black's prospects while enlarging White's. Black may answer with 2, but now White can turn his attention to the upper side or elsewhere, and because of White 1 it will not be hard for him to trim down Black's profit on the left side. Compare this with **Dia. 16,** where Black has pushed with 1 and 3 and greatly enlarged his territory. Black 2 in **Dia. 15** may not seem like much of an extension, but if Black plays 2 in **Dia. 17** he leaves White a good invasion point at 3, which aims at White 'h', which is related to White 'i'. Black 5 in **Dia. 16** was also related to White 'i'.

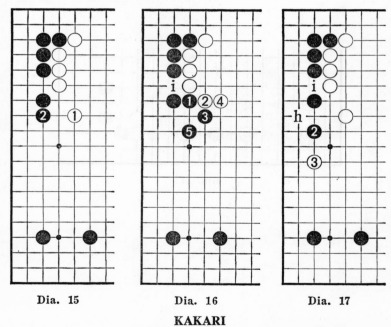

| Dia. 15 | Dia. 16 | Dia. 17 |

KAKARI

If a shimari is a good formation, then it stands to reason that a move which prevents the making of a shimari is good too. Such moves are called kakari, and the following are a few typical examples.

Dia. 18 shows the scene from an actual game between two professional players. White 1 was a kakari made to reduce a potentially large area, and after the moves up to Black 6 White felt satisfied with what he had accomplished and went to the upper side to make a big extension at 7. The sequence from 1 to 6 is what is known as a **joseki**, that is, a reasonable and fair pattern of play in the corner. There are innumerable joseki variations—in **Dia. 18** Black 6 might be omitted, or White 5 might be positioned differently, or Black 4 might be played at 'j', or White 3 at 'k', etc. Instead of White 1 there are also other ways to attack a stone on the 3–3 point, (e.g. 'k'), although they would not be appropriate

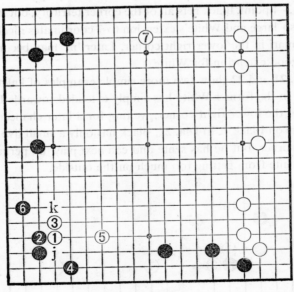

Dia. 18

here. We cannot do more in this book than give a few typical examples of the kinds of plays that are joseki.

The moves that immediately preceded White 1 in **Dia. 18** are shown in **Dia. 19**, and are one of the common joseki involving a stone on the 4–4 point.

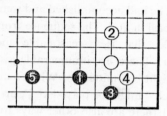

Dia. 19

Dia. 20 shows one of the many joseki developing from a stone on the 3–4 point. Black gets all of the corner territory, but it is not really so large and White's extension to 7 coordinates nicely with his shimari in the lower right corner. Later 'm' may become another good extension for White.

Dias. 21 and **22** show two more simple examples of kakari and joseki. In the former White has simply extended towards Black's stone in the lower right corner, waiting for a later chance to put pressure on Black 1. In **Dia. 22**, Black has only a small live group in the corner, but he has sente and can next play 'n', perhaps, to keep White from getting too much on the outside.

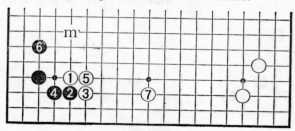

Dia. 20

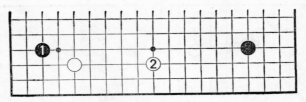

Dia. 21

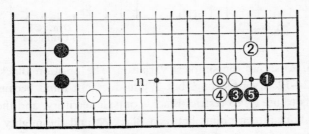

Dia. 22

THE 3–3 POINT INVASION

When your opponent has a stone on the 4–4 point, instead of making a kakari like 1 in **Dia. 19** there is another strategy you can follow. You can keep your distance from his stone and await a fitting opportunity to invade beneath it at the 3–3 point. By doing so you can consume the corner territory, although your opponent builds up power on the outside.

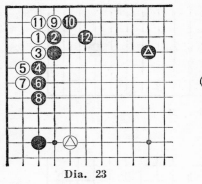

Dia. 23

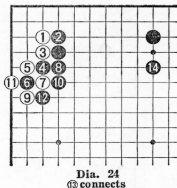

Dia. 24
⑬ connects

Dia. 23 shows the simplest variation. The position Black gets with 2—12 is very strong, but White does not mind because he expects to use ⊘ to restrict Black's outside territory, and there is only about fifteen points between Black ⬤ and the mighty wall.

Instead of playing 6 as shown in **Dia. 23** there is another possibility, as shown in **Dia. 24**. There Black uses 6 as a sacrifice stone so as to end in sente and play 14. (Because of this possibility White might do better to play a kakari at 7 instead of the invasion at 1.)

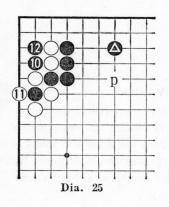

Dia. 25

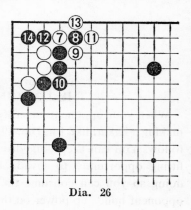

Dia. 26

Dia. 25 shows the same variation, except that now Black ⬤ is closer and a jump up to 'p' would not yield so much territory, so Black has played 10 to take the corner in gote. In **Dia. 26** White has played 7 and 9, threatening a double atari at 10, to avoid the sequences of the previous two diagrams. These joseki of the 3–3 point invasion are so important that they should be the first ones you learn.

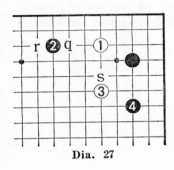

Dia. 27

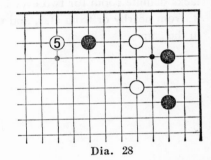

Dia. 28

HASAMI

Black 2 in **Dia. 27** is a hasami, that is, a scissors play, a move which attacks by preventing the opponent's extension along the side of the board. Against a hasami it is natural to skip toward the center, as with White 3, preparing to counter-attack on one side or the other, but as long as White has not established room for two eyes for his stones he will have to be careful, which is of course the idea behind Black 2. Black might play his hasami at 'q' or 'r' instead of at 2, or on the fourth line just below any of these three points. If Black played 'q', White would tighten up his formation by playing 's' instead of 3, while against Black 'r' he might make no answer at all. After **Dia. 27** White could continue with a hasami of his own, at 5 in **Dia. 28** for example.

MAKE TERRITORY WHILE ATTACKING

In go the best moves tend to be those which serve more than one purpose, and the fastest way to build territory is to do so while attacking. **Dia. 29**, which is borrowed from a professional game, shows this strategy in action. By playing 6 and 8 Black gained sure profit around the edges while undermining White's eye shape, and then he kept up the chase while defending his territory on both sides with 10 and 12. As long as the white group lacks definite room for two eyes Black can continue to threaten it, from nearby or from afar, and thereby maintain the initiative in the game.

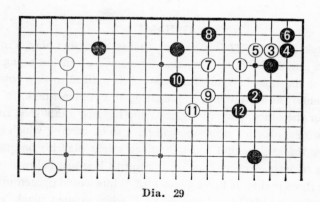

Dia. 29

THICKNESS

The white group in **Dia. 30** shows us one example of what is known in go as thickness. That is, White's stones display some outward-facing strength, with no weak points for Black to exploit. The fighting can rage around this group, but it will stand steady as a rock, and black stones may crash in ruin against it.

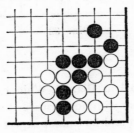

Dia. 30

There is a go saying, "Stay away from thickness", which tells how to play against thick positions. In **Dia. 31**, for instance, Black should extend no further than 1 or 'a', keeping a safe distance between his rather weak stones and his opponent's strong ones. After 1 he can next extend to 'b', approaching White's thickness cautiously, step by step.

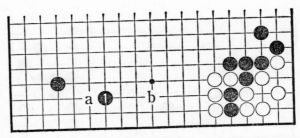

Dia. 31

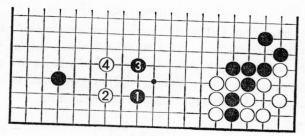

Dia. 32

If Black extends to 1 in **Dia. 32**, White can invade at 2. Now Black may well end up with no territory at all on the lower side, for his corner is open and he cannot expect to get much of anything in front of White's thick wall. White 2 and 4 may be left a bit weak, but so are Black 1 and 3.

It would be a grave mistake for White to play 2 in **Dia. 33**. White 2 is too close to White's own thickness and has much less value than Black 3. Even if Black fails to play 3 and White attacks by playing there himself, White 2 will turn out to be a comparatively worthless stone.

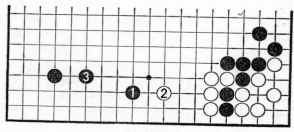

Dia. 33

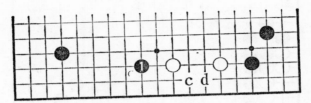

Dia. 34

In **Dia. 34,** however, the two white stones form a thin position, and Black is fully justified in extending all the way to 1. If attacked from above, it may be hard for White to find enough room at the edge of the board for two eyes, and Black can steal what space there is by playing 'c' or 'd'.

It is only common sense to drive your enemy toward your thick positions and away from your thin ones. In **Dia. 35,** for example, Black 1 attacks from the correct direction. Even if White extends to 2, his position is far from safe in the face of Black's thickness.

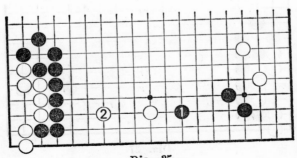

Dia. 35

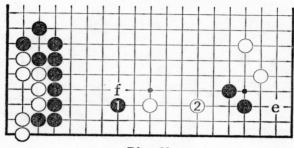

Dia. 36

In **Dia. 36**, however, Black's attack fizzles out after White 2, for White is threatening to play 'e' and Black must now make a defensive move. Nor is Black's profit on the left so big, for White can press at 'f' to narrow the territory in front of Black's wall.

White 2 in **Dia. 37** is another way to answer Black 1. It aims at White 'g', but Black can take profit with 3 and 5, the white group remains weak, and there is still a chance for Black to get territory on the left later.

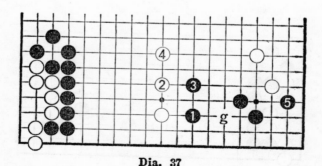

Dia. 37

You should not underestimate the power of thickness, for it is just as valuable to form thick, outward-facing positions which can be used for attacking as it is to stake out actual territory along the edges of the board. You must also beware of allowing your positions to become too thin, lest you constantly be forced to defend them while conceding territory to your opponent. It is particularly dangerous to have two very weak groups on the board, since if your opponent can find a move which attacks both of them simultaneously, one of them may die.

CHAPTER 11: RANKS AND HANDICAPS

One of the features of go is its handicap system, under which two players of widely disparate abilities can play games which are fair and interesting to both sides. Perhaps 50% of all go games are played with handicaps. A good way for a player to improve is to play handicap go against stronger players, so that he can learn their techniques at first hand.

When go is played without a handicap Black is thought to have an advantage of some five points, which is enough to be noticeable to strong players but is not decisive. If it is necessary for the weaker player to have a greater advantage, then instead of playing his first move wherever he likes he begins by placing from two to nine black stones on the board in a set pattern, as illustrated in one of the eight diagrams on the next four pages. (In the three stone handicap he places the third stone in his own lower right corner). Then White makes the first real move of the game, wherever he pleases, after which the two players take turns in normal fashion.

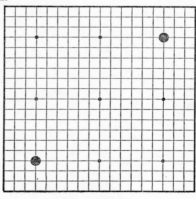

2-stone handicap

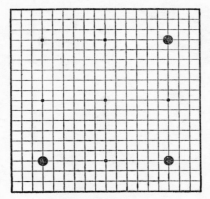

3-stone handicap

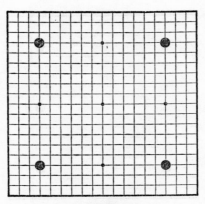

4-stone handicap

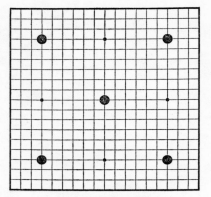

5-stone handicap

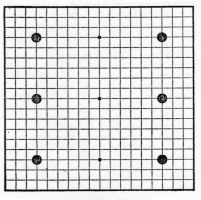

6-stone handicap

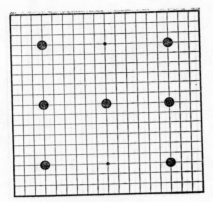

7-stone handicap

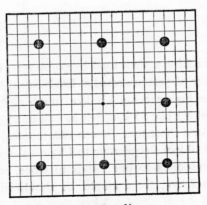

8-stone handicap

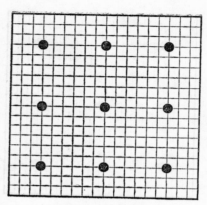

9-stone handicap

There is a ranking system used by go players, which works as follows. Weaker players are rated at levels called **kyu**, the weaker the player the higher being his kyu number. A raw beginner starts at something like 35 kyu, but he will quickly improve, and after playing for a short time, (about two months), he can expect to reach about 10 kyu. Progress up to 1 kyu is slower. Each step in this scale corresponds to one handicap stone, so that when a 2 kyu plays a 7 kyu, for example, he should give a five stone handicap. If a 2 kyu plays a 3 kyu then the latter receives no handicap, but takes the black stones every time.

Advanced players are similarly ranked into levels called **dan**, with the higher numbers now belonging to the stronger players. The next step after 1 kyu is 1 dan (called shodan in Japanese), followed by 2 dan, 3 dan, 4 dan, and 5 dan. Here again each step corresponds to one handicap stone, and the gap between 1 kyu and 1 dan also corresponds to one stone, so that in principle it is easy to determine the proper handicap between any two players of known ranks. Official ranks are granted by some of the national go organizations. The ranking system is the same throughout the world, although the values of the ranks naturally differ somewhat from place to place, and like currencies, they tend to suffer from inflation over long periods of time. The ranks used by professional players, by the way, are on a different scale. A professional shodan can give an amateur shodan about seven stones, while he receives no handicap from stronger professionals. The best players in the world are 9 dan professionals.

In non-handicap tournament games it is customary to nullify Black's advantage by subtracting 5½ points from his territory at the end of the game, a system which also prevents drawn games. These 5½ points are called **komi**. (In some tournaments the komi is 4½ points) To decide who will hold black in such games, one of the players picks up a small handful of white stones and his opponent calls, "even-sente", or "odd-sente". The stones are then counted by pairs, and if the second player has guessed even or odd correctly he receives black. Otherwise, he receives white. The same method can be used between two players of equal rank in friendly games.

CHAPTER 12: EXAMPLE GAMES

The following are two of the author's own games against other Japanese professional go players. In the first one the author was White while Black was Kitani Minoru, whose go school is currently turning out some of the best young players in Japan. This game was played in 1949, when both contestants were 8-dan, on June 8th and 9th.

FIGURE 1 (1-25)

The first twenty-four moves constitute the **fuseki,** in which both sides try for position and avoid sharp fighting. Kitani invaded at 25, so as to use his strength in the lower left corner and the thickness he had made with 17, 19 and 21, and the middle game began.

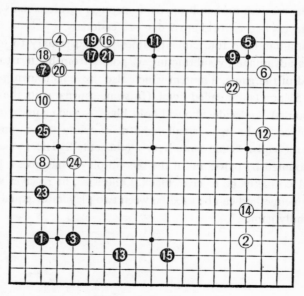

Figure 1 (1—25)

FIGURE 2 (26–48)

White 28 and 30 were inserted so that White could later play atari at 'a', which threat forced Black to play 37 instead of the more aggressive 'b'. That is, if Black played 'b', White would play 'c' intending next to cut at 37, and Black would have to defend. Black did not want to provoke White 'c', which would strengthen White in the center, so he simply defended at 37. White now came down on Black's stone in the middle of the upper side, and Black fought back vigorously there.

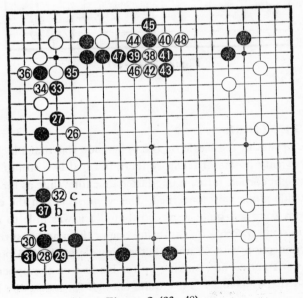

Figure 2 (26—48)

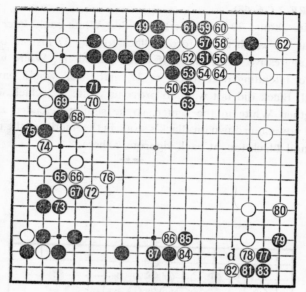

Figure 3 (49–87)

FIGURE 3 (49–87)

The upshot of the battle on the upper side was that Black kept about twenty points of territory there but lost two stones in the upper right corner, rather a good exchange for White as far as the upper side alone was concerned. The white stones in the center, however, were left quite weak, so that Black was able to attack them in sente with 65–76, capturing one of them and ensuring his own connection with 69 and 71, then invade at the 3–3 point in the lower right corner, making up for his loss on the upper side. Black's shape up to 79 is not quite enough for a sure life in the corner, but as long as the cutting point at 'd' remained White could not kill the black group. The intention behind White 84 and 86 was to cause fighting which would reinforce 'd' and would make use of the strength of 72 and 76.

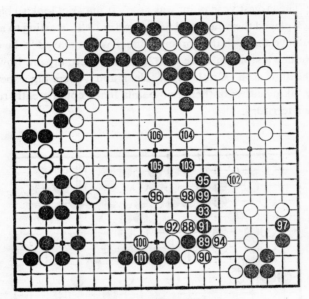

Figure 4 (88—106)

FIGURE 4 (88–106)

Black 97 assured the life of the corner group, but now White was hot on the attack in the center. He enlarged his right side in sente with 102, then gave chase with 104 and 106. Although he did not really hope to kill the black group, by attacking in this fashion he expected to solidify his own central position in sente, and this we shall see happening in the next figure.

FIGURE 5 (107–129)

Black skillfully managed to live in the center and trim down White's right side territory at the same time, but naturally he ended in gote. With the large scale fighting over, the game was now ready to enter the **yose** (endgame) stage, and it was White's move. The largest yose point was at 'e'. It may not look so big, but if Black played there he could next jump in to 'f', starting to attack White's eye shape in the corner, while if White played 'e' he could next rescue a stone in sente with 'g'. Even more urgent, however, was the atari at 'h'. On the right side 'i' and 'j' were big, especially 'i'. By taking either of these two points Black could greatly reduce White's territory.

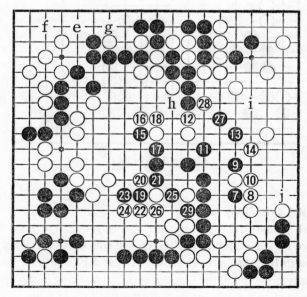

Figure 5 (107–129)

FIGURE 6 (130–156)

The largest yose points were taken in correct sequence in this figure. Notice how White played 32 while he could do so in sente, that is, before Black had a chance to capture one stone with 43 and 47. (If Black answered 32 with 'k', then White 33 would force a ko fight for the life of the corner.) Notice how White played 36–40 in sente before defending at 42 in gote. Notice also how Black played 37, threatening to continue with 38 and connect, before capturing at 41. Black 53 and White 54 were related to the threat of White 55.

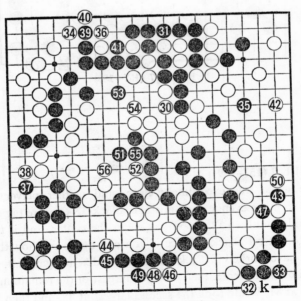

Figure 6 (130—156)

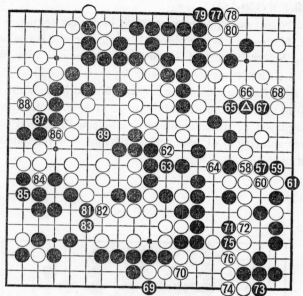

Figure 7 (157—189)

FIGURE 7 (157–189)

The game was exceedingly close, and neither player could afford to make even a small mistake. Black 57–61 were big on the right side, but then White 64 was big in the center, and it threatened to cut off Black ⬤. See if you can figure out how this cut would have worked if Black had failed to defend against it. Black played 67–79 in sente, then took the largest of the remaining yose points at 81. White took the second largest at 88, and then Black got the third largest at 89.

FIGURE 8 (190–215)

Black kept sente throughout this figure, although White did manage to slip in a couple of forcing plays of his own at 102 and 104. Finally Black connected at 115 in gote. Black 115, by the way, not only rescued Black 113 from capture but also kept White from invading the lower side at 'n'. White 'n' would not work because Black 'm' would be atari against thirteen stones in the center. At the end of this figure only small plays, worth one or two points apiece, were left, but the game was so close that even they were important.

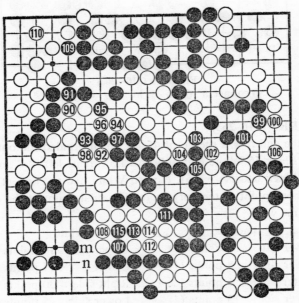

Figure 8 (190–215)

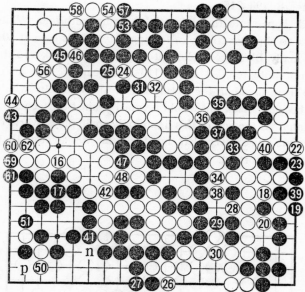

Figure 9 (216—263)

21 connects **49** ko **52** ko **55** ko **63** at **46**

FIGURE 9 (216–263)

In the end it was the ko at 45–46 which decided the outcome. After Black 55 White had only two ko threats left, ('n' and 'p'), while Black had 57, 59, 61, etc., so White had to connect at 56, losing one point of territory there. The final count at the end of the game was:

Black		White	
Lower left	35 points (1)	Upper left	16 points (1)
Lower right	8 points (1)	Center	11 points (2)
Center	6 points	Right side	30 points (1)
Upper side	13 points (4)	Lower side	5 points
	62 points		62 points

The numbers in parantheses are the numbers of prisoners already removed from the board which are being counted. Since each side captured two stones in the ko, they cancel out, and we don't bother to count them. White, however, had originally captured a stone at 56, which we do count. This long battle ended in a draw.

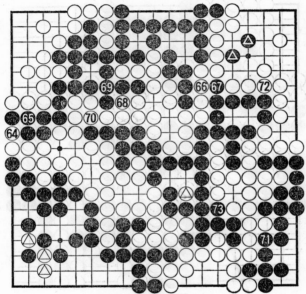

Figure 10 (264—273)

FIGURE 10 (264-273)

The moves in this figure show the neutral points being filled in. Although these plays gain no territory, Black must respond to 64 and 68. It makes no difference in what order the other moves are played. Finally the stranded stones, the two Black ●'s in the upper right corner and the three White ○'s in the lower left corner and the stone marked ○ in the center, are taken off the board and placed in the opponent's territory along with the other stones captured during the course of the game.

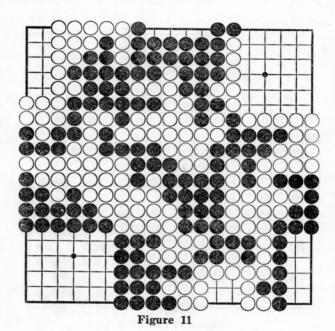

Figure 11

FIGURE 11

The dead stones have been removed, all the prisoners replaced on the board and the territories rearranged. That the score was tied is plainly visible.

EXAMPLE GAME 2

FIGURE 1 (1–25)

This game was played in 1926 between the author, then 6-dan, who held black, and Honinbo Shusai, 9-dan, one of the strongest players of this century. The first twenty-five moves are the fuseki, among which 6–9 and 17–21 are two simple joseki. After White 24 the author left the right side in order to defend his stone on the left while attacking the three white ones above it.

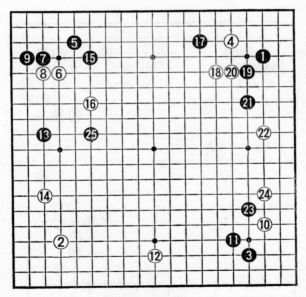

Figure 1 (1—25)

FIGURE 2 (26–50)

White counterattacked in the upper right corner with 26, and the middle game fighting began. When Black connected at 39 the ko lost its value, and White took sente on the upper side with 40.

Black 41 was a typical double-threat play, preparing both for an attack on the white stones in the upper right corner and for the invasion at 43. Black 43 turned out to be a sacrifice stone, but Black built thickness in the center with 45–49 and could later take the lower right corner by pushing through at 'a'.

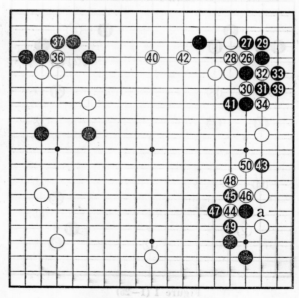

Figure 2 (26—50)
㉟ ko ㊳ ko

FIGURE 3 (51–76)

Black used his thickness by invading at 55 but White cut through his thin position on the left side with 56–60, and suddenly two weak black groups were under simultaneous attack. The one on the lower side got out into the open, but White 76 blocked the escape of the group on the left. This group was much too large to give up, so Black next had to make two eyes for it.

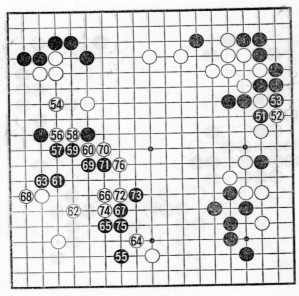

Figure 3 (51—76)

FIGURE 4 (77–102)

With the moves up to 95 Black lived on the left side. If Black 95 were omitted, by the way, White 'b' would kill the group. White naturally kept sente and returned to the unfinished business on the lower side, where the weak black and white groups began to fight against each other.

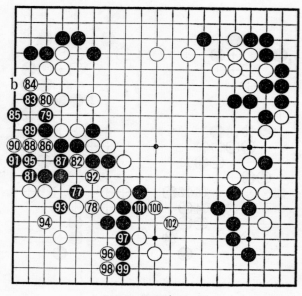

Figure 4 (77–102)

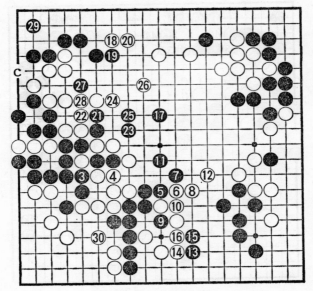

Figure 5 (103—130)

FIGURE 5 (103–130)

The black and white groups both got out into the center, and the fighting shifted to the upper left. Notice how Black took profit in sente with 13 and 15 before defending in the center with 17. Black attacked with 21–25, but White 26 surrounded his upper left corner group. White was now threatening to play 'c', after which he could either start a ko to kill the black group on the left side or play 29 to kill the one in the corner. Black had to defend at 29, and White chose to secure his lower left corner territory with 30.

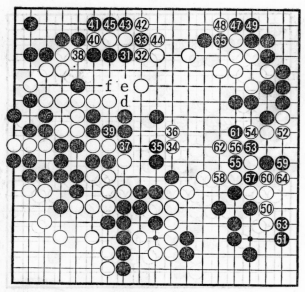

Figure 6 (131–165)
㊻ connects

FIGURE 6 (131–165)

The fighting became complicated; after 37, Black 'd', White 'e' Black 'f' was threatened, which would have cut off and killed the white group in the upper left—can you figure this out? White 38 defended, Black 39 secured the weak center group, and White 40 cut off and captured three black stones. White would have liked to answer Black 49 by connecting at 65, but then Black 50 would have decided the game. The sequence on the right from 52 to 64 was fairly complicated, but at the end of it the five black stones were almost dead. Even so, Black was doing well enough as he played 63, forcing White to answer at 64 and then made the large cut at 65. White had kept the initiative through most of the game, but Black had dodged his attacks and had enough territory left to win.

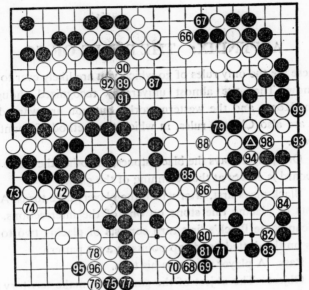

Figure 7 (166—199)
㊾ ko at ▲

FIGURE 7 (166–199)

When Black 99 rescued three stones out of the middle of White's territory on the right side, Honinbo Shusai gave up. If he had kept on by playing next at 94, the final score would have been:

Black		White	
Upper left	12–14 points	Upper side	14–19 points
Upper right	17 points	Lower left	25 points
Lower right	15–19 points	Right side	6 points
Left side	16 points	at most	50 points
about 63 points			

APPENDIX: THE RULES OF GO

These are the only rules of go which you are likely ever to need to know. They are almost universally recognized thoughout Japan, Korea and the western world, but you are warned that there are also Chinese rules, in which the method of counting is different.

1.   One player plays the black stones, the other the white ones. The board is empty at the beginning of the game.

2.   Black plays first, after which the players take turns. A turn consists of placing one stone on one of the intersections. In a handicap game Black's first turn consists of placing two to nine stones on the dotted handicap points in a set pattern.

3.   **Pass**   A player may pass his turn.

4.   **Object**   The object of the game is to make territory (surrounded vacant points). The winner is the player with the most territory at the end of the game. If both have the same amount, the game is drawn.

5.   **Capture**   A stone or group of stones of one color is captured and removed from the board when all the points adjacent to it are occupied by enemy stones.

6.   **Counting**   One point is subtracted from a player's territory for every captive he loses.

7.   **Ko**   A player cannot immediately recapture in ko.

8.   **Suicide**   A player cannot capture his own stones.

9.   **End**   The game ends by mutual agreement when neither player can gain any more territory or prisoners.

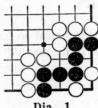

Dia. 1

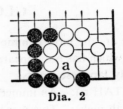

Dia. 2

10. **Dead stones** Stones which cannot possibly evade capture are removed as captives at the end of the game.

11. **Bent four in the corner** The black stones in **Dia. 1** are dead. (See page 85).

12. **Seki** No points are counted in a seki.

13. **Ko** must be connected at the end of the game. In **Dia. 2**, for instance, White must connect at 'a' (or capture the black stone) no matter how many ko threats he has. **Dia. 3**, which is seki, is an exception to this rule.

14. **Triple ko** In positions such as **Dia. 4**, (Black to play), if neither player is willing to give up the local fight the game is cancelled—neither won, lost nor drawn. Triple ko is extremely rare. There are a few more, even less likely, ko-like situations to which the same rule applies.

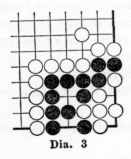

Dia. 3

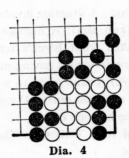

Dia. 4

GLOSSARY

These are the most commonly used technical go terms, including one which has not appeared so far in the text. All of them are originally Japanese words.

atari (a TAH ri):   An immediate threat to capture.

dame (dah meh):   This word, which is Japanese for useless, has two meanings in go:

1.   A neutral point, territory for neither player.
2.   A liberty (defined on page 12).

dan (dahn): A rank given to stronger players.

fuseki (f' SEH key):   The opening maneuvers of the game, up to the point where the real fighting begins.

geta (geh tah):   The method of capture described on page 62.

gote (go teh):   A move which loses the initiative; the opposite of sente.

hasami (ha SAH mee): A scissors play, or squeeze play. See page 107.

joseki (jo seh key):   An established pattern of good play in the corner.

kakari (kah KAH ree): A move attacking a single stone in the corner.

ko (koh):   A situation involving unending capture and recapture.

komi (koh mee): A number of points, (usually $5\frac{1}{2}$), sometimes subtracted from Black's territory at the end of the game to compensate for his having moved first.

kyu (kyu) A rank given to weaker players.

me ari me nashi (meh AH ree, meh NAH sh'): A semeai in which one side has one eye.

oiotoshi (oyo TOE sh'): The method of capture described on page 74.

seki (seh key):   An impasse situation in which groups live without having two eyes.

semeai (seh meh eye):   A battle between two adjacent groups, neither of which can form two eyes.

sente (sen teh):   A more which keeps the initiative by forcing the opponent to answer.

shicho (shi CHO):   A zig-zag pursuit in which the pursued group is kept in atari.

shimari (sh' MAH ree): A 2-stone corner enclosure.

shodan (sho dahn): 1 dan, the lowest dan rank.

yose (yo seh):   The end game, in which only small-scale engagements are fought.

NATIONAL GO ASSOCIATIONS

These are organizations set up to serve the increasing number of go players in various parts of the world. They serve their members by organizing go events, publishing magazines, supplying books and equipment as well making publicity directed at the general public. The reader will find them especially useful for making contacts with other players in his district.

ARGENTINA: Asociacion Argentina de Go,
Casilla de Correo 63, Martinez, Buenos Aires.
(contact: Mr. Franco Liceni, secretary)

AUSTRIA: Osterreichischer Go-Verband
Geylinggasse 17/9, 1130 Wien
(contact: Mr. Alfred Nimmerrichter, president)

CANADA: Canadian Go Association
5212 King Edward St, Montreal 265, Quebec.
(contact: Mr. Harry H. Schwartz, president)

CZECHOSLOVAKIA: Czech Go Association
Laubova 8, Praha 3
(contact: Dr. Dusan Prokop, president)

FRANCE: Association Francaise de Go
Boite Postale 95–06, Paris 6e,
(contact: Mr. Patrick Merissert, secretary)

F. R. GERMANY: Deutscher Go-Bund e.V.
8032 Lochham bei München, Ahornstr. 12
(contact: Mr. Karl-Ernst Paech, president)

GREAT BRITAIN: The British Go Association
60 Wantage Road, Reading Berks RG3 2SF
(contact: Mr. Derek Hunter, secretary)

HOLLAND: Nederlandse Go-Bond,
Johannes Verhulstraat 125, Amsterdam.
(contact: Mr. Jan van Frankenhuysen, secretary)

JAPAN: Nihon Ki-in (The Japan Go Association)
7–2, 5 Bancho, Chiyoda-ku, Tokyo
(contact: Foreign Dept.)

KOREA (South):	Hangook, Kiwon, 13–4 Kwanchul Dong, Chongroku, Seoul (contact: Mr. H. R. Lee)
TAIWAN:	China Wei-chi Association, 107 Kwaing St., Taipei (contact: Mr. C. K. Ing)
U.S.A.:	The American Go Association, 21 Sunset Drive, Summit, N.J. 07901 (contact: Dr Robert M. Ryder, president)
YUGOSLAVIA:	Go Zveza SR Slovenije, Ljubljana, Cankarjeva 1-1, PB 298 (contact: Dr. Lovro Sturm, president)

Go Clubs

The club list below is by no means exhaustive but is made up of the most important clubs found in the major population centers in each country. For more complete details of go clubs in your country or for more up-to-date information write to your local go association (see the previous section).

ARGENTINA
Buenos Aires Go Club,
c/o Franco Liceni,
Casilla de Correo 63,
Martinez, (Bs. As.)

AUSTRALIA
Sydney Go Club,
c/o K. Flatow,
15 Chisholm Rd,
Belmore 2192, N.S.W.

Chess Center of S.A.,
102 Gawler Place,
Adelaide 2000, S.A.

AUSTRIA
Go Klub Daikoku,
Rolf Wessely,
Sensengasse 5, 1090 Wien

Go Klub Ebisu,
Peter Sussner,
Löwengasse 49/18, 1030 Wien

Go Klub Kuro-Shiro,
Herbert Florian,
Florianigasse 66/6, 1080 Wien

Linzer Go Klub,
Hans Jüngling,
Merianweg 33, 4020 Linz.

BRAZIL
Brazil Nihon Kiin Chapter,
Av. Liberdade 486, 2–SL,
São Paulo.

CANADA
Montreal Go Club,
H.H. Schwartz,
5212 King Edward St,
Montreal 265, P. Quebec.

Toronto Go Club,
J.E. Williams,
90 Forest Grove Drive,
Willowdale, Ont.

Ottawa Go Club,
Y. Tsuchiya,
2140 Fillmore Crescent,
Ottawa 9, Ont.

University of Alberta Go Club,
Dr C.J. Elliott,
Dept of Physics, Univ. of Alberta,
Edmonton, Alberta.

Winnipeg Go Club,
Y. Tsutsumi,
88 Glenlawn Ave, St Vital,
Winnipeg 8, Manitoba.

CHILE

Chile Nihon Kiin Chapter,
J. Maeda,
Embajada del Japon, Santiago.

DENMARK

Københavns Go Klub,
M.E. Larsen,
Popple Alle 16,
DK–1890 Hareskov.

F.R. GERMANY

Go Zirkel Berlin,
Gerhard Benkmann,
Lindauerstr. 7, 1 Berlin 30

Berliner Go-Verband,
Fritz John,
Berlin 15, Emserstr. 14.

Go-Verband Düsseldorf,
Ratbod Freiherr v. Wangenheim,
4032 Lintorf, Duisburgerstr. 27.

Hamburger Go-Club,
Hans Geisler,
Beim Strohhause 14,
2000 Hamburg 1.

Go-Gruppe in Frankfurt,
Kurt Dueball,
Humboldstr. 22, 6000 Frankfurt.

Go Gruppe in Hannover,
Winfried Dörholt,
3001 Wulferode, Am Felde 5.

Bayerischer Go Verein,
Karl-Ernst Paech,
8032 Lochham bei Munchen,
Ahornstr. 12.

FRANCE

Paris Go Club,
Café Le Trait D'Union,
122 Rue de Rennes, Paris 6e.

Marseilles Go Club,
M. Alexander,
88 Rue Grignan,
13000 Marseilles ler.

GREAT BRITAIN

London Go Club,
Dr Geoffrey Gray,
88 Beaufort St, London SW 3.

Bristol Go Club,
A.H. Smith,
55 Heath Road,
Downend, Bristol BS16, 6HD.

Reading Go Club,
Derek Hunter,
60 Wantage Road,
Reading, Berks RG3 2SF.

Edinburgh University Go Club,
John E. Allen,
40 Bryce Crescent,
Currie, Midlothian,
Edinburgh EH14 5LL.

Leeds Go Club,
J.D. Thewlis,
213 Hyde Park Road, Leeds 6.

Manchester Go Club,
J. Payne,
24 Victoria Avenue,
Didsbury, Manchester M20 8RA.

HOLLAND

Amsterdamse Go Club,
Jan van Frankenhuysen,
Joh. Verhulststraat 125,
Amsterdam.

Leiden Go Club,
J. van Rongen,
Hoge Morsweg 111, Leiden.

Rotterdamse Go Vereniging,
C.P.A. Put,
Keplerstraat 57, Spijkernisse.

Groningse Go Club,
Wim Klein-Haneveld,
Donker Curtiusstraat 131,
Hoogezand.

Drienerlose Go Vereniging,
R. Steen,
Calslaan 5-206, Enschede.

Nijmegen Go Club,
M.E.C. Jansen,
Prof. Huybersstraat 139,
Nijmegen.

JAPAN
Nihon Kiin Kaikan,
7-2 Gobancho, Chiyoda-ku,
Tokyo

HUNGARY
Budapest Go Club,
Lászlo Béla Kovács,
Budapest V, Molnár-u27, III, 11.

PARAGUAY
Paraguay Nihon Kiin Chapter,
T. Ishida,
Casilla de Correo 34,
Encarnación.

PERU
Peru Nihon Kiin Chapter,
M. Kamisato,
Jilon Cangallo 441, Lima.

IRAN
Teheran Nihon Kiin Chapter,
I. Ushioda,
PO Box 11-1739, Teheran.

RUMANIA
Clubul de Go Timisoara,
Dr. Ing Pilz Iosif,
Timisoara III,
Str. Brâncoveanu 14.

SWITZERLAND
Geneve Go Club,
Service d'Information,
Consulat-General du Japon,
16 Place Langemalle, Genéve.

Schweizer Go Club,
Erwin Siegrist,
CH 4058 Basel, Schleifenstr. 40.

U.S.A.
New York Go Club,
23A West 10th St.,
N.Y., N.Y.

Princeton Go Club,
Prof. Ralph Fox,
134 Cedar Lane,
Princeton, N.J. 08540

Murray Hill Go Club,
Kurt Nassau,
1 B 310 Bell Tel. Labs,
Mountain Ave,
Murray Hill, N.J. 07974

Baltimore Go Club,
Robert Gross,
3401 N. Charles St, Apt 607,
Baltimore, Md. 21218

Greater Washington Go Club,
Arthur N. Lewis,
11530 High View Avenue,
Silver Spring, Md. 20902

Massachusetts Go Association,
William Mann,
63 Botolph St,
Melrose, Mass. 02176

Ann Arbor Go Club,
James Kerwin,
441 South First St,
Ann Arbor, Mich. 48103

Chicago Go Club,
Gene Edlin,
1255 Sandburg Terrace, Apt 2709
Chicago, Ill. 60610

Univ. of Chicago Go Club,
John Raz,
5463 S. University Ave,
Chicago. Ill. 60615

Carleton College Go Club,
Arthur Gropen,
Carleton College,
Northfield, Minn. 55057

Univ. of Wisconsin Go Club,
Ismat S. Baba,
813 Witte Hall,
Madison, Wis. 53706

Purdue Go Club,
S. Gartenhaus,
Physics Dept, Purdue Univ,
Lafayette, Ind. 47907

Denver Nihon Kiin Chapter,
Roy S. Tani,
1944 Larimer St,
Denver, Colorado 80202.

Last Exit Go Club,
3930 Brooklyn N.E.,
Seattle, Washington.

Portland Go Club,
Doug Cable,
6550 S.W. Vermont,
Portland, Oregon 97223

Berkeley Go Club,
Herb Doughty,
2612-B Hillegasse,
Berkeley, Calif.

San Francisco Go Club,
1881 Bush St,
San Francisco, Calif. 94109

Los Angeles Go Club,
Richard Dolen,
2329 Kansas,
Santa Monica, Calif. 90404

La Jolla Go Club,
Peter Preuss,
Mathematics Dept. UCSD,
San Diego, Calif.

Hawaii Kiin,
K. Ota,
982 Prospect St,
Honolulu, Hawaii 96822

YUGOSLAVIA
Go Društvo Ljubljana,
Lovro Sturm,
Cankarjeva 1–1, PP 298,
Ljubljana, Slovenija.

Go Savez Hrvatske.
Masarykova 13,
Zagreb, Hrvatska.

GO EQUIPMENT

The Basic Go Set (BS. 1) $18.80

This consists of a good quality folding wooden board, 1.5 cm in thickness, with a full-size playing surface and a complete set of black and white glass stones, 5.0 mm thick. They are attractively packed in a sturdy cardboard box, and the price includes surface mail postage to any part of the world. This set is perfect for beginners.

For those who wish to indulge in a higher quality set, The Ishi Press also supplies thicker one-piece boards, with or without legs, wooden go bowls for holding the stones, a variety of go stones of different sizes, including the expensive black slate and white clamshell types, and portable magnetic go sets.

Orders for the Basic Set (BS.1), together with payment, or enquiries about the other equipment, should be sent to **THE ISHI PRESS, INC., CPO BOX 2126, Tokyo, Japan**

GO BOOKS

G9 Go para Principiantes (paper) **$2.00**
  by Kaoru Iwamoto

A Spanish translation of **Go for Beginners**.

NK2 Go Proverbs Illustrated (hard cover) **$5.50**
  by Kensaku Segoe, honorary 9-dan

In the 4,000 year history of go, many useful sayings have been coined to teach the basic principles. In this book the study of go is organized around the application of these go 'proverbs'.

G2 Basic Techniques of Go (hard cover) **$6.60 0–87040–161–0**
G2p Basic Techniques of Go (paper) **$3.60 0–87040–162–9**
  by Haruyama, 6-dan and Nagahara, 4-dan

Contains a survey of the basic tesuji, the techniques, strategies and joseki of handicap go and an introduction to the end-game. Written by two young internationally-minded Japanese professionals, this book has enjoyed acclaim from all over the world ever since it was first published.

G6p Strategic Concepts of Go (paper) **$3.60**
  by Yoshiaki Nagahara, 4-dan

The beauty and focal point of go is to be discovered in its strategic rather than tactical side. Here then are the eight fundamental strategic concepts presented in book form for the first time, providing a framework in which all aspects of go may be placed. The senior companion to 'Basic Techniques of Go', this book also contains an extensive problem section to test the reader's newly acquired understanding.

G5 The Middle Game of Go, Vol. 1: Eio Sakata
              (cloth cover) **$6.00 0–87040–164–5**

This is the sequel to Modern Joseki and Fuseki, in which four top games played by Eio Sakata, 9-dan are presented. Expand your knowledge of the middle game of go by studying Sakata's own move-by-move commentary.

G7 Championship Go, Vol. 1:
The 1971 Honinbo Tournament (cloth)   **$8.00**   0-87040-165-3
by **Kaoru Iwamoto, 9-dan**

In 1971, the 22-year old Yoshio Ishida battled his way to the top of the Honinbo League and then went on to overcome the mighty Rin Kai-ho in the title series to become the new Honinbo. This excellent book charts Ishida's progress with detailed analysis of 14 of his games.

NK3 Vital Points of Go (Spiral binding)   **$5.50**
by **Kaku Takagawa, 9-dan**

One's progress in go depends a great deal on developing a good intuition. The go board is too wide and the game too profound for one player to think out every move logically and accordingly feeling plays a large part. Takagawa sets out to help the reader improve his perception and thus give a sound base from which intuition can operate.

G4 GO: International Handbook and Dictionary -2nd edition, revised and expanded 1972 (paper cover)   **$2.00**   0-87040-163-7

This book contains a wealth of information for all players. Most important is the illustrated dictionary of more than 200 go terms defined in both English and German to help the player decipher Japanese go texts. In addition, there is a list of all the professional players with their rankings, a description of the major tournaments, title holders-past and present, the professional promotion system, go throughout the world, etc.

The Ishi Press Elementary Go Series
G11 (Vol. 2) 38 Basic Joseki (paper)   **$3.75**
by **Kiyoshi Kosugi and James Davies**

A vivid, one-volume survey of the entire field of joseki, describing the principal variations of the thirty-eight most common corner patterns with unforgettable clarity, pointing out the key ideas in each, and showing how to choose and use joseki in relation to other stones on the board. 244 pages—597 diagrams—diagrammatic table of contents—illustrated glossary of technical terms.

All the books, with prices attached, may be ordered by sending payment (postage is included in the price) to:

THE ISHI PRESS, INC., CPO Box 2126, Tokyo, Japan